S0-EAX-961

Questions and Answers on

EXECUTIVE COMPENSATION

HOW TO GET WHAT YOU'RE WORTH

GRAEF S. CRYSTAL

PRENTICE-HALL, INC., Englewood Cliffs, New Jersey

For T. P. B.

© 1984 by PRENTICE-HALL, INC.,
Englewood Cliffs, New Jersey

All rights reserved. No part of this book
may be reproduced in any form or by any means
without permission in writing from the publisher.

Library of Congress Cataloging in Publication Data

Crystal, Graef S.
    Questions and answers on executive compensation.

    Includes index.
    1. Executives—Salaries, pensions, etc.—Miscellanea.
I. Title.
HD4965.2.C79   1984   658.4'0722   84-11630

ISBN 0-13-748476-3

ISBN 0-13-748468-2 {PBK}

Printed in the United States of America

PRENTICE-HALL INTERNATIONAL, INC., *London*
PRENTICE-HALL OF AUSTRALIA, PTY. LTD., *Sydney*
PRENTICE-HALL CANADA, INC., *Toronto*
PRENTICE-HALL OF INDIA PRIVATE LTD., *New Delhi*
PRENTICE-HALL OF JAPAN, INC., *Tokyo*
PRENTICE-HALL OF SOUTHEAST ASIA PTE. LTD., *Singapore*
WHITEHALL BOOKS, LTD., *Wellington, New Zealand*
EDITORA PRENTICE-HALL DO BRASIL LTDA., *Rio de Janeiro*

CONTENTS

SECTION TWO: SHORT-TERM INCENTIVES **27**

- Is there any advantage to using company shares to exercise a stock option rather than paying cash?   67
- Does every stock option plan contain a stock-for-stock exercise provision?   68
- If one doesn't already own enough shares with which to make a stock-for-stock exercise, may he or she make a partial option exercise and then turn around and use the newly acquired option shares to make a second stock-for-stock exercise?   68
- If the FMV drops substantially below the option price, will the company consider reducing the option price to give a second chance to reap some gain?   69

Incentive Stock Options **69**

- What is an *incentive stock option* (ISO)?   69
- What will be the option price of an ISO?   70
- How long does one have to exercise an ISO?   70
- What happens if employment is terminated?   70
- May an individual exercise various options in any order desired?   70
- If one is blocked from exercising an ISO, what about cancelling the earlier grant?   71
- What if the second option grant is not an ISO grant, but rather an NQSO grant?   71
- Does one have some sort of tax obligation when the ISO is exercised?   71
- Does this mean that if one can avoid the alternative minimum tax, he or she will pay no tax whatsoever in conjunction with the ISO exercise?   72
- What happens when the ISO shares are sold?   72
- If ISOs are so good, why not grant only ISOs and forget about granting further NQSOs?   73
- How can the government make money on an ISO grant compared to an NQSO grant and yet limit the size of an ISO grant compared to an NQSO grant?   75

Stock Appreciation Rights **75**

- What is a *stock appreciation right* (SAR)?   75
- Who gets SARs?   76
- How does an insider get cash for an SAR?   76

TABLE OF EXHIBITS

WHY THIS BOOK IS NEEDED

Not too many years ago, executives were paid quite simply. They received a base salary, perhaps some sort of discretionary bonus at the end of the year, and, if they kept their noses clean for many years, a gold watch and a small annuity.

Times have changed. Today there are many new forms of compensation to be added to a base salary, a bonus, and a pension. We now have stock options, performance shares, performance units, restricted shares, deferred compensation, a wild variety of perquisites, and an equally mystifying menu of supplemental fringe benefits.

At the same time, the complexity of the forms of compensation being offered to executives has increased tremendously. In the old days, you were told, "Do a good job, and we'll see." If you did a good job, you saw, or at least that was the theory, some sort of bonus. Now bonuses in many companies are governed by elaborate formulas that even Einstein might not comprehend instantly.

Large corporations have both internal and external compensation advisors when it comes to designing various forms of executive compensation. Indeed, I am one of them. So, in that sense, the corporation is well served with experts.

But the poor executive often has no advisors or, worse, advisors who are not true experts in executive compensation. To be sure, he can turn to his tax person and learn about the tax consequences of various forms of executive compensation. But the tax person isn't going to know why the company installed that form in the first place, what it is intended to do, and, most important, how the executive can maximize his pretax income (which is one handy way to maximize after-tax income!). Or, he can turn to his lawyer and learn about the various legal ramifications. But his lawyer may also not be schooled in what the company is truly trying to achieve.

A free market operates best—and perhaps only—if there are informed buyers and informed sellers on both sides of the transaction. As noted, there's little question that the buyers of executive talent are well informed. But there's also equally little question that most of the sellers—the executives themselves—are ill informed.

The purpose of this book, then, is to try to remedy this imbalance so that in the future the sellers can be virtually as well informed as the buyers.

To corporate managements, an attempt to improve the knowledge of the sellers of corporate talent may seem like heresy. They may fear that executives, if armed with some knowledge, will merely become even harder bargainers than they are now. But the sword cuts both ways. If a company is trying to convince an executive that some form of compensation is worth a fortune when it really isn't, perhaps this book will cause the company some pain. On the other hand, many companies are today offering truly magnificent incentive opportunities to their executives, and yet many of them, because they are not informed, are not in a position to appreciate what is already on their plate. From that perspective, therefore, an informed seller of talent may make it easier for the company to strike an amicable, and reasonable, bargain.

In the chapters that follow, you will get a pretty good grounding in all the basic forms of executive compensation, including base salaries, short-term incentives, long-term incentives, deferred compensation, perquisites, and supplemental fringe benefits. The only elements missing from this discussion are so-called broad-based fringe benefits—fringe benefits that, like pensions, savings plans, group medical insurance, and group life insurance, are extended on a nondiscriminatory basis to all, or almost all, employees, as opposed to a small group of more senior executives. Happy reading.

Graef S. Crystal

SECTION ONE

BASE SALARIES

The most fundamental of all compensation elements is base salary. In one sense, your base salary should be fairly easy to determine. All the company need do is find out what other companies pay for comparable work and then offer the same amount of money. But did you know that:

- You can increase your pay if you can increase the number of employees working for you (or for your subordinates).

- You can increase your pay if you can convince your superiors that you should report at a higher level of the organization, even though your job is exactly the same as it was before.

- You can increase your pay by quitting and joining another company.

- If you have a Harvard MBA, you can flaunt your education. But over the long run, you probably won't get any more money than the person who went to State U. and holds a position comparable to yours.

- It costs a lot more to live in New York City than in Houston. But if you think those tight-fisted New York employers are going to pay you more to compensate for the higher cost of living, forget it.

- It isn't just New York City employers who are tight-fisted. Living costs in Los Angeles are reported to be as high as those in New York, while living costs in Atlanta are much lower than in Los Angeles. Yet Los Angeles employers aren't going to give you any more sympathy—or pay—than their Atlanta counterparts.

- For a while, it didn't make much difference what industry you worked in as far as figuring your pay was concerned. But now, industry pay differentials have reemerged with a vengeance.

- You should fight for the highest salary grade you can get, even though your pay may be so low right now that you aren't even at the minimum of your current salary range.

- Not all companies are skinflints. A fair number set out quite consciously to pay a premium to the market.

- You may receive regular merit increases, but chances are that most of the increase has nothing to do with "merit."
- Performing outstandingly may help you get a promotion, but it's unlikely that you'll be paid a lot more than someone with decidedly canine characteristics.

Is there any benefit to me from my company's having a systematic, rather than an ad hoc, approach to salary administration?

In most cases, the answer is a decided yes. Without a systematic approach to establishing proper base salaries, there is a higher probability that you might end up being paid less than the true "going rate" for your responsibilities, and/or that you might end up receiving less than another executive in your own organization who has been assigned comparable responsibilities.

The output of a systematic approach to salary administration may consist of various policy statements, but its prime symbol is a salary structure.

What is a salary structure?

A salary structure consists of a number of salary grades, with each grade being assigned a minimum salary level and a maximum salary level.

Why have a salary structure?

For two reasons. First, as mentioned, to provide a systematic means of assuring that executives, and other employees as well, receive levels of pay that approximate some desired positioning vis-à-vis those companies your company considers appropriate to track.

The second reason is to achieve a measure of what might be called internal equity, a fancy name for keeping peace in the family. Hence, it is not only important that you believe you are being paid competitively, it is also important that you believe your pay is fair in relation to the pay of your peers within the company.

If a company has forty grades in its salary structure, does salary grade 40 have the highest range?

That is the case most of the time. Among other things, this approach fits neatly into the American conception that bigger is better. It also permits you to bandy about your grade number as a way of disseminating instant information about your level within the company. In that sense, salary grade numbers have status implications.

Every so often, however, a company reverses the salary grade order, such that the CEO is in salary grade 1. Even though things are upside down in that company, you'd be amazed at how quickly the players adapt to standing on their heads.

How does a company go about assigning an executive to a given grade?

There are many different approaches used. But two are by far the most popular. One involves the use of a so-called *point-factor system*. And the other involves the use of what is termed *slotting*.

How does a point-factor system work?

A point-factor system rests on the assumption that there are certain attributes, or factors, for which a company should pay. For example, you would agree with the proposition that, other things being equal, a position requiring an MBA is more responsible, and hence should carry greater salary, than one requiring only a BA. By the same token, you would also agree that, other things being equal, the need to have ten years of experience makes a position more responsible than one requiring only five years of experience.

The first thing the designers of a point-factor system do is determine how many factors the system will have. Few systems have fewer than three factors, although some may have upwards of ten factors. The most widely used point-factor system, the Hay system, has three factors (know-how, accountability, and problem solving).

The next thing the designers must do is identify levels of responsibility within each factor. For example, in working with a factor like education, you might specify that the lowest level of responsibility requires a high school diploma and that the highest level requires a Ph.D. In between, you might set up road stops for AA's, BA's and MA's. By the same token, your experience factor might start out with one year of experience at the lowest level of responsibility and move up in a series of levels to fifteen years of experience.

Next, the designers assign a maximum number of points to each factor. In so doing, they implicitly give one factor greater weight than another. Suppose, for example, that there are three factors in the particular plan and that the designers assign a maximum point value of 1500 to the first factor, 1200 to the second, and 800 to the third. Since there are a maximum possible 3500 points that can be earned and the first factor offers a maximum point value of 1500, then the first factor carries 42.9 percent of the total weight. In contrast, the third factor, which carries a maximum point value of only 800, carries only 22.9 percent of the total weight.

Finally, the designers assign point values to each level of responsibility within each factor. Suppose here that Education is assigned a maximum point score of 1500. In that case, the maximum point score might be reserved for a position requiring a Ph.D. degree. In turn, a position needing only a high school diploma might be assigned an education point score of only 100. And the need for a BA degree might carry 500 points.

So there you have it! Having designed the point-factor system, the company proceeds to evaluate every position on every factor. Then the various point scores are totalled to produce a total point score for the position.

How does the point-factor system designer know what to do?

One isn't sure! Some designers justify their system on the basis that the various points and factors have a high correlation with the way executives are actually paid. Some other designers justify their system, not on the basis that executives are really paid the way the system implies, but that executives should be paid according to the designer's conception of the ideal world. And in still other companies, no one really knows the answer to this question. The company has had the same system for eighty years. And the designer, though perhaps not those people now using the system, is resting in peace.

How does the company determine what a point is worth?

By selecting a number of benchmark positions and then surveying the competition.

What is a benchmark position?

A benchmark position is any position the duties and responsibilities of which can be found at many other companies. Thus, the position of CEO is a classic benchmark position because, in the final analysis, you either run the company or you don't.

In selecting benchmark positions, a company must take pains to avoid comparing positions simply on the basis of title. For example, the position of chief financial officer is usually considered to be a benchmark position, because virtually every company has one. But one company's CFO may be missing the important treasury function (the treasurer reports directly to the CEO), while another company's CFO not only has all the traditional CFO functions (controller, treasury, MIS) but also supervises the heads of legal, personnel, and public relations. In such a situation, it wouldn't make sense to lump either of these executives in with more traditional CFO positions.

On the other hand, there are many positions in a company, indeed maybe even most positions, that cannot be compared externally because they contain a custom mix of duties and responsibilities. We will see what happens to these positions momentarily.

Who are the competitors?

Take the case of a $3 billion food company. In structuring its pay packages, it could, alternatively, measure its pay levels against those of:

- Any other company, regardless of industry, of about the same size. Thus, it might compare itself to any company whose sales volume was in the $2 to $4 billion range.

- Any other company, regardless of industry, of about the same performance. Thus, if its after-tax return on equity was 17 percent, it could measure itself against all other companies whose after-tax returns on equity were in the 15 percent to 19 percent range. This would not only include companies in other industries but also companies of greatly different size. Or the measure of performance might be growth in earnings per share (EPS), rather than after-tax return on equity.

- Any other company in the food business, regardless of the size of that company.

- Any other company in the company's geographic location.

- Ideally, any other company in the food business, in the company's geographic location, with $2 to $4 billion of sales, and with about the same after-tax return on equity and growth in EPS. Probably, however, you will find precious few fish in that particular net.

- Any other company that is in the same size range and that is in the same general type of business. For example, a food processing company is basically engaged in consumer package goods marketing and hence might properly be compared to other companies that, though not in the food processing business per se, are engaged in consumer package goods marketing.

As you can see, there are many ways to answer the question: Who are our competitors? And, depending on how you answer this critical question, you will get vastly different results.

What are some of the factors that influence competitive pay levels?

The CEOs of General Motors and the Keokuk Mattress Company probably have the same job descriptions. But most people would readily agree that the CEO of GM should be paid more than his Keokuk counterpart, because GM is such a huge company.

So right away, we know that the size of the company is one factor that influences pay. To illustrate, suppose our hypothetical food company with $3 billion of sales decided to test the pay practices of twenty-five companies with sales ranging from $100 million to $4 billion. Suppose further that the position being tested is the CEO.

Exhibit 1 shows, in tabular form, the salary levels of each of the twenty-five CEOs. It also shows the median CEO to be earning a salary of $400,000 and the average CEO to be earning a salary of $375,000. Now one way to obtain the going rate for a CEO would be to use the median or average salary.

But there is also another way. Exhibit 2 shows what happens when we portray the twenty-five-company data in graphic form, with

**EXHIBIT 1   Base Salary of Chief Executive Officer
in Twenty-five Hypothetical Companies**

COMPANY	SALES VOLUME[a]	CEO'S SALARY[a]
1	$100	$200
2	$250	$225
3	$300	$175
4	$400	$250
5	$600	$300
6	$800	$225
7	$850	$400
8	$950	$350
9	$1,000	$375
10	$1,100	$315
11	$1,250	$380
12	$1,350	$400
13	$1,500	$365
14	$1,700	$425
15	$1,900	$450
16	$2,100	$380
17	$2,300	$400
18	$2,500	$425
19	$2,700	$450
20	$3,000	$500
21	$3,200	$475
22	$3,400	$450
23	$3,600	$480
24	$3,800	$500
25	$4,000	$490
Average	$1,786	$375
Median	$1,500	$400

[a]In thousands of dollars.

the horizontal axis representing sales volume and the vertical axis representing salary. Right away, you can see that there is some relationship between sales volume and salary; as the sales volume rises, so does the salary.

Exhibit 3 shows the same scattergram as Exhibit 2, but this time a line of best fit has been drawn through the twenty-five dots. By reading this line at $3 billion of sales, you can see that the going rate of salary is

EXHIBIT 2 Base Salary of Chief Executive Officer Versus Sales (Hypothetical Data)

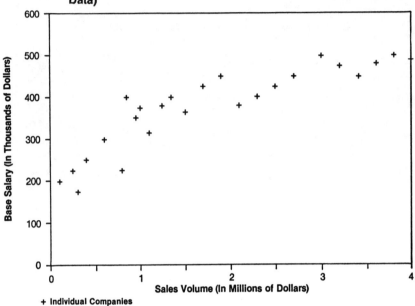

EXHIBIT 3 Base Salary of Chief Executive Officer with Line of Best Fit Inserted (Hypothetical Data)

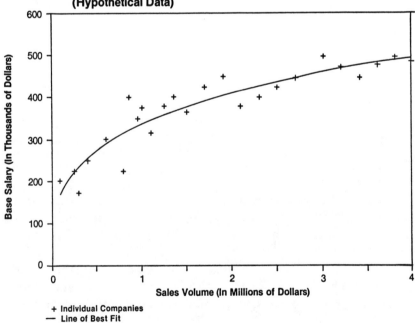

about $460,000. This value, of course, is significantly higher than the value derived from taking the simple median or the simple average of the twenty-five salaries.

So which is the correct figure? All are correct in a technical sense, but the figure derived from the line of best fit on the sales volume graph is the most correct, because it better helps to explain why one CEO in the twenty-five-company group is paid more than another.

In this case, therefore, we know that the twenty-five different salary levels were not obtained by looking in a table of random numbers. There is indeed some rhyme and reason to the way these particular CEOs are paid—the size of the company.

At the same time, however, you can observe that the twenty-five dots do not all lie on the resulting line of best fit. There are factors other than sales volume operating to determine why CEOs are paid differently. What are some of these factors?

- *Assets.* Other things being equal, the greater the level of assets in the company, the greater the level of pay. Hence, a company with $3 billion of sales and $3 billion of assets is apt to pay more than a company with $3 billion of sales and $1.5 billion of assets.

- *Profits.* Other things being equal, a company with higher profits is apt to pay somewhat more than one with lower profits. However, the relationship is not as strong as some would like to believe, and this is particularly true when it comes to base salary (as opposed to other forms of compensation, which are more heavily influenced by profitability).

- *Number of employees supervised.* Other things being equal, the greater the number of employees one supervises, either directly or through subordinates, the higher the pay. So, if there is a fairly weak relationship between profits and pay and a fairly strong relationship between number of employees supervised and pay, your desire to maximize your income would suggest that a bit of empire-building is in order, even if that doesn't do much for profits.

- *Board membership.* If you're not the CEO or the chief operating officer (COO) (almost automatically a member of the board) getting a seat on your company's board of directors isn't merely a tonic for your ego. It carries real dough as well. Being on the board means one of two things. It means you have a really heavy-hitting position. Or it means that you are a superlative performer and are destined for greater things. Probably, it means both things at once. And because it does, it deservedly entitles you to higher pay.

- *Organization reporting level.* If you can't convince your CEO that you should get a seat on the board, at least try to make him see the merits of having you report directly to him. Other things being equal, your level in the organization will have a material influence on your pay. This is because almost every organization operates on a hierarchical pay principle, which dictates that a boss must make more than his or her subordinates.

- *Number of subordinate managerial levels.* A while back, we said one way to get more pay is to beef up the number of people you supervise. Now let's refine that a bit. The novice pay maximizer will try to get 100 employees under his or her command and have all of them report directly to him or her. But the master pay maximizer will get 100 employees under his or her command and have them report to him or her through four subordinate levels of management. The master pay maximizer knows that the hierarchical pay principle just noted will operate to produce a higher pay level for him or her than would be the case with a more egalitarian form of organization.

- *Age of the executive.* You'll probably find it easier, and a lot more fun as well, to pad your organization with extra subordinates than to somehow make yourself older. But if you're so inclined, getting older does carry at least some rewards.

- *Time in position.* If you aren't promoted very frequently, you can take a bit of solace from the fact that, other things being equal, the longer you have held your current position, the more you will be paid.

- *Length of service with the company.* Being the great loyalist you are, you probably think that your years of service with your current employer will result in higher pay. Wrong! The studies show that, other things being equal, the longer you have been with your company, the less you will be paid. Suppose all companies had exactly the same pay structure. That being the case, each company would try to offer, say, its controller the same salary of $100,000. Now go on to suppose that Company A lusts after Company B's controller and tries to get her to switch employers. Company A offers Company B's controller a salary of $100,000, only to find that she is already earning that salary. So its lust still unabated, Company A takes a deep breath and offers Company B's controller $130,000 in order to get her. Well, Company A's new controller has zero length of service with Company A when she first joins the Company. And she is paid $130,000 per year salary. And all her peers in Company A are paid only $100,000. And all her peers have a lot more service than she does. And you figure it out!

- *Education.* Education makes a difference early in one's career. But over time, the effects of education tend to disappear. Consequently, having a Harvard MBA *may* propel you into the CEO's chair one day. But when you get there, you'll find that the CEO across the street, who barely graduated from high school, is earning just as much.

- *Geography.* New York City has an extremely high cost of living and extremely high tax rates. Houston has a lower cost of living and very low tax rates. Therefore, other things being equal, one would think an executive working in New York earns more than one working in Houston. It may make sense to believe that, but it's wrong! Studies often report that the average New York executive earns more than the average Houston executive. But those studies are biased. The fact is that the average company in New York is bigger than the average company in Houston. Hence, it is size that accounts for the difference in pay, not geographic location. Why, you may ask, will an executive work in New York for the same pay as he could earn in Houston, if his or her standard of living will be lower? One theory has it that there are nonpay attributes that attract people to New York, for example, the Metropolitan Opera, the great museums, and so forth. Another theory states that New Yorkers are not happy unless they are miserable. Hence, the filthy streets, the foul air, and the probability of getting mugged all contribute mightily to generating the desired feelings of misery. So New Yorkers are either culture lovers or masochists, depending on which theory you want to accept. Based on the author's experience with New York, New Yorkers are both culture lovers and masochists.

- *Type of industry.* Until shortly after the end of World War II, executives rarely moved from industry to industry. Indeed, the premium on loyalty being what it then was, executives rarely moved from company to company within the same industry. As a result, different industries frequently exhibited considerably differing pay levels. Then came a surge in the demand for executive talent and the beginnings of a belief that a good executive in one industry could transfer his skills to another industry with a minimum of fuss. At the same time, we saw the emergence of the executive recruiter. All these factors combined to cause a dramatic change in behavior on the part of many, indeed most, executives. No longer was it unthinkable to move from one company to another within the same industry. No longer was it even more unthinkable to move from one industry to another. Executives were for sale to the highest bidder. Over time, executives used their own bodies to arbitrage away many industry pay differentials. Their constant movement from one industry to another caused previously lower-paying industries to jack up their rates and previously higher-paying industries to moderate the growth of their rates. This trend reached its peak just before the onset of the recession beginning in 1981–82. By that point, it was impossible to demonstrate true interindustry pay differentials, except for such crazy industries as the entertainment industry (which marches to its own drummer, who, doubtless, also earns 300 percent more than other drummers). Even the once-prosaic banking industry started to pay its executives more like mainline industrial companies (although it hadn't quite closed the gap). Then came the most severe recession since the Great Depression. Companies in such stricken industries as steel, aluminum, housing, and autos didn't just slow down the growth in pay levels. They didn't even go so far as to freeze pay levels. They cut them! Yet in other industries, which breezed through the recession fairly unscratched, it was business as usual. Although pay didn't rise at its former rate, it rose nonetheless. As a result, there has been a reemergence of industry pay levels. Whether the new pay differentials will remain a permanent fixture of the pay landscape remains to be seen. But it behooves the executive to consider the pay climate in a given industry before deciding to cast a lot with that industry.

- *Supply and demand.* Ultimately, of course, this factor accounts for all differences in pay. In the 1930s, when the ability to sell goods to people who had no money to buy them was highly prized, the marketing executives in industrial corporations earned more than their counterparts in manufacturing and finance. In the 1940s and 1950s, when the ability to produce goods that had a ready market, no matter what their quality or price, was highly prized, the manufacturing executives earned more than their counterparts in marketing and finance. In the 1960s, 1970s, and early 1980s, when the ability to raise capital in tight markets and the ability to keep large organizations from spinning out of control was highly prized, it was the financial executive who earned more than his counterparts in marketing and manufacturing. We have also witnessed the rapid rise of the computer executive and a bit more pay for the personnel executive. This is due to a greater governmental intrusiveness and a belated understanding that the quality of a company's human resources does make something of a difference. Indeed, we may yet come full circle because the threat from low-priced, high-quality Japanese goods is acting to place a premium on executives who know how to manufacture such goods.

After that windy digression, once again, how do you determine the value of a point?

Suppose a company has 100 executive positions, which have each been assigned a number of points. Suppose also that the company has identified twenty-five of those positions as being suitable benchmark positions. Finally, suppose that the company selects an appropriate group of comparator companies and finds out what each of them pays in salary to each of the twenty-five benchmark positions.

Exhibit 4 is a scattergram showing the intersection of each position's number of points and its going rate of salary among the comparator companies. It can be seen at a glance that there is quite a good relationship between the number of points assigned to a particular position and its going rate.

Exhibit 5 takes the scattergram of Exhibit 4 and shows the line of best fit. This line of best fit in turn represents what the typical company would offer in salary to an executive with a given number of position evaluation points.

So there you have it. In theory, you can determine a fair market rate for any position simply by reading the line of best fit at the number of points assigned to that position. For example, by looking at Exhibit 5, we know that the going rate for a position carrying 6000 position evaluation points is $115,000. Note here also that the line of best fit can be applied to even the most customized positions for which valid market readings cannot be directly obtained.

EXHIBIT 4   Point-Factor Evaluation (Hypothetical Data)

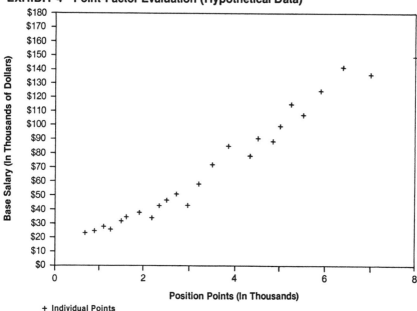

+ Individual Points

EXHIBIT 5 **Point-Factor Evaluation (Hypothetical Data)**

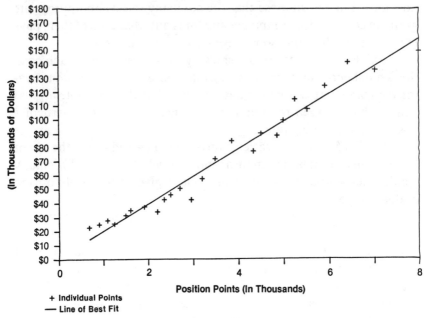

Does that mean that the company will have a different salary grade for each different point value?

It may mean just that in some companies. Thus, if one more point is worth only $50 per year, at the margin, then having one more point will put you in a different salary grade with a minimum and maximum that are $50 per year higher.

Most companies, however, admit that determining the worth of a position is not an exact science. Accordingly, they band groups of points together into salary grades. For example, a company might decide that all positions having point values in the 951–1000 range will be assigned to the same salary grade, while all positions having point values in the 1001–1050 range will be assigned to the next higher salary grade. In essence, the company is saying that no one is calibrated closely enough to truly distinguish between the worth of two positions having point values that are within fifty points of each other.

How many grades does the structure have?

Every field has its own "theology," and the field of compensation is no different. Some compensation "theologians" are of the opinion that there should be few grades in a structure and that everyone of them should have some positions assigned. Others think that there should be many grades in a structure and that it makes little difference whether a given grade has no positions assigned to it.

As a practical matter, it really matters little what the "theologians" think. What is of real importance is what grade you are assigned to and what that grade's salary range is.

A while back, you mentioned that there was a second way to assign positions to salary grades. What is it?

Many companies don't want to bother with designing a point-factor evaluation plan and then assigning points to each executive position. Instead, they simply:

- Identify a number of benchmark positions. This step is no different from that used by companies with point-factor plans.

- Determine through a survey the market value of each benchmark position. Once again, this step is no different from that used by companies with point-factor plans.

- Develop a salary structure around the benchmark positions. That is, the company develops what it sees as the correct number of salary grades and then assigns each benchmark position to that salary grade, the midpoint of which closely approximates the market value of the position. To illustrate, suppose that salary grade 15 carries a midpoint of $80,000 and salary grade 16 carries a midpoint of $90,000. If a benchmark position is determined through a survey to have a market value of $86,000, it will likely be assigned to salary grade 16.

- Compare each nonbenchmark position to various relevant benchmark positions. On that basis, a grade assignment is determined judgmentally for each nonbenchmark position, and the position is slotted into that grade. In effect, the company is reasoning that if A equals B and A equals C, then B must equal C. Thus, if a benchmark position should be in salary grade 16 because of market considerations, and if another nonbenchmark position carries substantially the same amount of responsibility as the benchmark position, then that nonbenchmark position should also be assigned to salary grade 16.

This process of slotting is not as elegant as that involving the design of all sorts of factors and points. But it seems to get the job done in many companies and to produce end results that are not materially different from those that would have been obtained through a point-factor system.

You keep talking about obtaining pay data from your competitors. Why would a competitor even want to give you the time of day, much less reveal its innermost pay secrets?

All companies are in the same boat when it comes to establishing pay levels. They all have to be in the position of assuring their shareholders that they are not paying unreasonably high amounts of compensation. Yet they also have to be able to attract and retain capable executives.

Years ago, it was thought that you could steer the compensation boat by looking at turnover figures. If your turnover was almost nonexistent, that probably meant you were paying too much and could start to hold down the growth of pay levels. Or, if your turnover was exceedingly high, that probably meant you were paying too little and should start to raise pay levels.

There may be something to this theory, but, unfortunately, turnover is what the economists call a lagging indicator. Thus, by the time turnover drops to almost zero, it may take years of slow pay growth to get down to a competitive position. Or, by the time turnover rises to high levels, it may take years of effort to rebuild your executive team.

It is not infrequently the case that warring nations will reluctantly declare a short truce and then resume hostilities. That is exactly what happens concerning the exchange of pay data among archenemies.

Typically, however, exchanges of pay data are accomplished through third parties, such as consultants, survey groups, trade associations, and the like. The typical ground rules of such surveys require that no company receive back any information that would let it identify the actual pay practices and pay levels of any other single company in the survey. By the same token, no other company is able to view your own pay data. But all companies benefit by getting some sense of the overall pay market through various published averages, medians, trend lines, and so forth.

Earlier, you mentioned the term "midpoint." What is the significance of the salary range midpoint?

Mathematically, of course, a salary range midpoint is nothing more than the average of the range's minimum and maximum figures. In the world of compensation, however, the salary range midpoint takes on almost mystical significance. It generally symbolizes what the company intends to pay a fully satisfactory, but not above-average, performer.

On that basis, therefore, paying below the salary range midpoint is usually reserved for below-average performers or for executives who are new to the position. And paying above the salary range midpoint is usually reserved for above-average performers.

At the same time, the salary range midpoint generally represents the market rate for the position. Hence, as mentioned earlier, if a position is a benchmark and the going rate is, say, $100,000, then that position will generally be assigned to that salary grade, the midpoint of which is as close to $100,000 as you can get.

You keep talking about going rates. Does that mean all companies strive to pay the average?

In a word, no! To be sure, the term *going rate* is synonymous with the average, whether the average is obtained by using simple statistics, reading a trend line from a chart, or employing highly sophisticated multiple regression techniques. But it does not follow that every company desires to anchor its salary range midpoints to the going rate.

It is theoretically possible for a company to decide that it wishes to be a low payer and therefore to anchor its salary range midpoints to, say, the 25th percentile of the comparator group distribution (a point where, in a group of 100 companies, seventy-five pay more than you do and twenty-five pay the same or less). If, say, the 25th percentile of the distribution is reached by offering 15 percent less pay than the average company, then this company would assign the position with a going rate of $100,000 to a salary range midpoint of around $85,000. Here, however, we stress the word *theoretically*, because it is the rare company that articulates a formal policy of paying below the average. There are, of course, companies that do pay below the average, or else the average could not be what it is. But whether they get there through sophistry or self-delusion, they will nonetheless look you straight in the eye and tell you that it is their policy to pay fully competitive rates.

On the other hand, there are a fair number of companies that articulate a formal policy to be above-average payers of compensation. You hear fairly frequently about a given company aiming to match the 75th percentile of the distribution. In that case, the company is saying that it wishes its pay levels to be exceeded, not by half the companies in its comparator group, but rather by only one-quarter of the companies. If the 75th percentile is reached with a premium of, say, 15 percent, then the benchmark position with a going rate of $100,000 will be assigned to that salary range midpoint that closely approximates $115,000.

Some critics of executive compensation contend that asymmetrical pay policies have the effect of unwittingly driving up pay rates. Thus, if no companies desire to be below-average payers, two-thirds of companies desire to be average payers, and one-third of companies desire to be above-average payers, then pay rates will constantly keep ratcheting up. Perhaps this is true, but the argument in some way denies the free will of any company to change its pay policy and not to follow slavishly (at least for a while) what is happening in the marketplace.

Academic arguments notwithstanding, you should know that there are quite a few companies out there who aim to pay a premium to the market. And, other things being equal, wouldn't you want to work for one of those companies?

How wide is a salary range apt to be?

That depends on the position level and on the company's policy. The most frequent practice is to structure a salary range such that its maximum is 50 percent higher than its minimum. Hence, a salary range with a minimum of $100,000 will likely carry a maximum of $150,000. In turn, that means that the maximum will be 20 percent higher than the midpoint, thereby creating a 20 percent premium for above-average performance. Some companies, however, like to have broader ranges, so the maximum might be 60 percent above the midpoint.

Other companies increase the range spread at higher and higher levels. Thus, a low-level managerial position might be assigned to a salary grade the maximum of which is 40 percent above the minimum. But a senior executive position might be assigned to a salary grade the maximum of which is 60 percent above the minimum.

As long as I haven't reached the maximum salary in my range, does it really make that much difference what salary grade I am assigned to?

You bet it does! From a practical standpoint, the closer you are to the maximum, the more difficult it will be to get a decent increase. In a way, the maximum is just like a metal median barrier on a divided highway. You use it for guidance, but you also keep a comfortable distance away from it.

On that basis, the best position to be in is to be assigned to a salary grade the minimum of which exceeds your current salary. In that case, there will be great pressure on the company to rectify the perceived inequity and to do so sooner rather than later.

In many companies, the particular salary grade to which you are assigned can trigger various levels of extra compensation. Hence, if you are in, say, salary grade 15, you may be entitled to receive an annual bonus equal to 15 percent of your salary in an average year, but if you are in grade 16, the comparable bonus level is 20 percent of your salary. By the same token, the normal stock option grant for someone in grade 15 may be 1000 shares, while for someone in grade 16 it may be 1200 shares. So you can see that the particular salary grade to which you are assigned can make a substantial difference.

How does the company go about determining what sort of salary increase I will receive?

Most companies start the process by establishing a salary increase budget for the year. Typically, this budget, which is stated as a percentage of payroll, excludes promotional increases but includes all other increases.

The first thing a company does in arriving at a budget figure is to measure its current salary levels against those being offered by the companies in its comparator group. At the same time, it tries to ascertain what those same companies are planning in the way of increases for the forthcoming year.

Finally, the company takes into account economic forecasts concerning the economy as a whole (and especially the predicted inflation rate), as well as its own likely profit levels during the forthcoming year. (This last factor usually carries relatively little weight compared to the other factors, except when the company finds itself *in extremis*.)

Putting all these factors together, the company sets a salary increase budget figure. If the company finds itself to be lagging behind the comparator group companies, the budget figure will be somewhat higher. Or, if the word is that other companies will be spending less next year than they did the year before, the budget figure will be somewhat lower.

While setting its salary increase budget for the forthcoming year, the company also usually confronts the issue of how much, if any, it should adjust its salary ranges. Typically, the figure selected will be smaller than that adopted as the salary increase budget figure. This is because a company can spend, say, 8 percent of payroll on salary increases and yet find that its overall average salary did not rise 8 percent by the end of the year. Rather, retirements and other forms of turnover acted to limit the rise to, say, 5 percent to 6 percent.

In making adjustments to salary structures, do companies incorporate expectations of what other companies will be doing during the forthcoming year?

Suppose a company determines through a survey that it should raise its salary structure by 10 percent in order to produce new midpoints that will approximate current competitive salary levels. Suppose also that the company, through the same survey, gains the impression that most of its competitors will be spending around 10 percent on salary increases during the forthcoming year. That being the case, what are the options?

- The company can increase its salary structure by 10 percent. Here, the company will be competitive at the beginning of the year, but, as the year progresses, its salary ranges will fall further and further behind the pay levels of the competition. By the end of the year, the salary structure will lag the market by approximately 8 percent. (As noted above, spending 10 percent on salary increases generally results in a lesser rise in average salaries.)

- The company can increase its salary structure by 18 percent. Here, the company aims to be fully competitive at the end of the forthcoming year. At the same time, it will be more than competitive at the beginning of the year—by about 8 percent.

- The company can increase its salary structure by 14 percent. Here, the salary structure will ride above the market by about 4 percent at the beginning of the year and will fall below the market by about the same 4 percent at the end of the year. Theoretically, it will equal the market around the middle of the year.

Different companies select different options, but few choose the most costly second option.

If I receive an 8 percent merit increase, is all of that increase really a merit increase?

Not at all! Companies may euphemistically speak about having an all-merit-increase program, but in reality the true merit increase portion of your overall salary increase is limited to the amount by which the increase exceeds the increase that would be needed to keep your salary in line with the salaries being paid by other companies. Or, to put it another way, your true merit increase is the amount by which your actual increase exceeds the amount necessary to keep you in the same relative position within your salary range.

Think of this process as being like gaining market share. If your competitors all increase their sales 10 percent, and you do the same, you have assuredly experienced a 10 percent increase, but your market share is the same as it was last year. It is only when you increase your sales by more than 10 percent that you begin to gain market share.

In that sense, therefore, you can get a better sense of what your bosses think of you if you do two things. First, subtract from your actual salary increase percentage the percentage adjustment in the salary structure. This is your true merit increase percentage. Second, determine the distance you have moved within the salary structure. For example, your previous salary may have been equal to 80 percent of last year's maximum for your salary range, while your new salary turns out to be 83 percent of this year's maximum.

Will my current salary range positioning have any influence on the salary increase I receive?

If your company is putting its money where its mouth is, it should. A while back, we mentioned that the salary range midpoint, in most companies, represents the ideal salary range positioning for a theoretical average performer. By the same token, the salary range maximum represents the ideal salary range positioning for a walk-on-the-water type, while the salary range minimum represents the ideal salary range positioning for executives imbued with canine characteristics.

It follows, therefore, that if you are judged to be an outstanding performer and if you are also situated at the bottom of the salary range, then you will have to receive an outsized increase to get you to where you belong, the maximum of your salary range. Hence, if the salary range minimum is $100,000, maximum is $150,000, and your superiors think you are marvelous, then, logically, your next increase should be for $50,000, thereby positioning you where your performance demands—at the maximum of the salary range. If you think that's going to happen, however, you're also the type who believes in the tooth fairy!

To be sure, if you really are low in your range but high in your performance, you may receive a larger-than-average increase, but it will probably fall way short of getting you where you should be. For example, if the salary structure is increasing 5 percent and the company is spending 8 percent of payroll on merit increases, you might receive an 11 percent salary increase, but, probably, things aren't going to get much heavier than that. Now consider that you are at the minimum of your range and that the maximum is 50 percent higher than the minimum. Given that your salary is advancing 6 percent faster than the structure itself, how many years will it take before you finally reach the salary increase maximum? Eight years!

At the same time, the company's pronouncements that no average performer will be permitted to advance past the salary range midpoint should also be taken with a grain of salt. Most companies don't have the will to implement their pronouncements; therefore, even an average performer is likely to make it to the maximum of the range, given enough time. Here, however, it may take twelve years, rather than eight years, to get there.

All of this suggests that, in most companies, there is relatively little relationship between salary range positioning and actual executive performance. Rather, there is a strong relationship between salary range positioning and the length of time the executive has held the position.

So, unless you are employed by the rare company that espouses a pay-for-performance principle in salary administration and then follows it, you will have to look elsewhere for the rewards that you deserve.

Why don't executives receive cost-of-living increases? After all, they are affected by price increases, too.

Most companies hate the thought of giving an across-the-board increase to any group of employees. They may get forced into accepting such a procedure when the employees are unionized, but they aren't going to budge an inch unless they have to. As a result, it is the rare company that will grant a cost-of-living increase to a group of executives.

That doesn't mean, however, that executives are not compensated for increases in the cost of living. When the cost of living rises, unions typically react by demanding higher wage increases (either in the form of cost-of-living escalators or simply out-sized wage adjustments). When those increases are granted, pay compression begins to develop. Hence, whereas a foreman earned 15 percent more than his average subordinate before the increase, he or she now earns only 5 percent more. In theory, if enough compression develops, then higher-level employees will refuse to work for their current pay. This in turn alters the supply-demand balance and results in increased pay levels for such employees.

At the same time, most companies have some sense of fair play. If they are forced to grant cost-of-living increases to unionized workers, they may react by increasing the size of their salary increase budgets for other employees—and well before greater discontent and higher turn-over would otherwise occur.

However a company gets there, adopting a higher salary increase budget when the cost of living is rising has the effect of protecting executives from changes in cost of living. The only difference, then, is that the protection comes in an indirect form (a larger annual increase), rather than in a more explicit form (a formal payment triggered by a change in the Consumer Price Index).

SECTION TWO

SHORT-TERM INCENTIVES

This section explores the first of two major incentive devices—short-term incentives. Did you know that:

- If you can convince your superiors to assign you to a higher salary grade, you will likely receive a larger bonus, even though your salary may remain unchanged.
- The more you make in base salary, the higher will be your bonus expressed as a percent of base salary.
- Not all companies that offer low bonus opportunities can be considered chintzy.
- Just because a company has low, or even no, profits for a particular year does not mean that there will be no money available for bonuses.
- Chances are that the performance of the division of which you are a part will have little or no impact on the size of bonus you receive for a particular year.
- Chances are that your personal performance contributions will count for little in the determination of how large a bonus you get.
- Many companies give you the opportunity to defer part or all of your bonus and then go on to offer very attractive returns on your deferred monies.

What is a short-term incentive plan?

A short-term incentive plan is designed to reward performance accomplishments in a single year.

What's the difference between a bonus plan and an incentive plan?

Some people believe that a bonus plan is one that operates like a sort of high-level profit-sharing plan, while an incentive plan offers a true incentive to improve results over time.

Some bonus plans are true incentive plans, and some incentive plans operate like profit-sharing plans. Therefore, we attach absolutely no significance to the two terms. They are interchangeable and will be so used in this book.

How many companies have short-term incentive plans?

Virtually all major companies have a short-term incentive plan, and the great majority of smaller companies do also.

Who is eligible to participate in a short-term incentive plan?

Eligibility varies. A few elitist companies restrict eligibility to a handful of senior executives—say, twenty-five executives in a company with $5 billion of sales. Going to the opposite extreme, a few egalitarian companies extend eligibility to employees earning base salaries as low as $25,000 per year.

Typically, however, a company is at neither extreme. A large company, for example, extends eligibility to around 1 percent of its total employee population. Thus, if the company has 80,000 employees, then around 800 executives are included for eligibility. Smaller companies have fewer eligibles, but the percentage of eligibles of the total employee population is likely to be higher than for large companies.

How do I get to be eligible for my company's plan?

Most companies have formal rules governing who gets into the short-term incentive plan. A few companies specify a dollar-salary test. For example, you will be in the plan if your base salary is $40,000 or more per year. Companies in this category always have lots of problems. First, when they increase the salary cutoff, as well they should in an environment where all salaries are increasing, they get criticized for taking something away. Second, two executives can be in the same salary grade, yet one can be in the short-term incentive plan, while the second is denied eligibility because his or her salary is just below the cutoff. (This result is sometimes defended on the basis that the executive with the higher salary is also the better performer and hence is more deserving of eligibility. But, as we have seen, there is usually little correlation between position in the salary range and executive performance.) Third, the dollar cutoff approach invites all sorts of games playing. The company, for its part, will try to hold a person just below the cutoff for as long as it can. For his or her part, naturally, the person will try like mad to cross the line, even if only by one millimeter.

A second approach to defining bonus eligibility involves the use of the salary grade. For example, the company may decree that any person who is assigned to salary grade 15 or higher will be eligible to participate in the incentive plan. Here, you can immediately see the importance of being assigned to the right grade. Even though you may have plenty of room to expand your salary, being assigned to a lower grade may rob you of eligibility to participate in your company's bonus plan.

Salary grade cutoffs are usually more fair. And the company is not put in the position of being a heavy as it is with the dollar-salary-cutoff approach. After all, by continuing to define eligibility as salary grade 15 or higher, the company automatically ratchets up the dollar-salary level required for eligibility every time it increases the overall salary structure. Of course, there will still be games playing galore even with a salary grade cutoff. The company will typically resist a salary grade assignment that just makes the eligibility cut, while the individual will push just as hard in the opposite direction.

A third approach involves the use of both salary grades and your level in the organization. For example, the company may extend eligibility to anyone who is assigned to salary grade 14 and higher and who is also in the top three levels of management subordinate to the CEO, as well as to anyone who is in grade 17 and higher, regardless of that person's level in the management hierarchy. This approach may prove useful in including more managers in the plan and fewer technical specialists.

What is a norm award?

A company will typically establish a norm award or a standard award for each eligible salary grade. Like the salary range midpoint, a theoretical construct is involved here. The norm award is that award payable to an average performer in a year where both the performance of the company and the performance of the profit center to which the individual is assigned are also considered average.

In theory, therefore, the sum of the salary range midpoint and the norm award are supposed to put the company where it wants to be vis-à-vis the comparator group. To illustrate, suppose that the typical comparator group company offers an executive in a given job a combination of base salary and short-term bonus equal to $135,000. If your company has established a salary range midpoint of $100,000 for this particular position, then it will likely accompany that salary range midpoint with a norm award of 35 percent of salary.

How do norm awards vary?

Within a single company, norm awards typically increase as a function of increasing base salary or salary grade. Indeed, the rate of increase is generally faster than the increase in salary, such that the norm award, expressed as a percentage of·salary, rises as the salary rises. This can be seen in Exhibit 6, which shows the norm award practices of one typical company.

EXHIBIT 6 Bonus-to-Salary Ratios (Typical Company Practice)

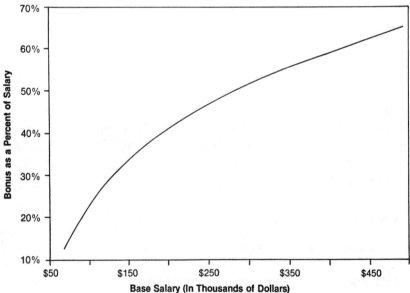

Note, however, that although norm award percentages rise with rising salaries at almost every company, there can still be huge differences from one company to the next. For example, the auto companies, in their salad days, used to think nothing of offering senior executives a bonus equal to 200 percent of their salary. And that was for a so-so year! In a great year, the bonus jumped to 300 percent of salary. On the other hand, there are companies whose idea of a norm award for the CEO is only 25 percent of salary, with lower executives receiving comparably lower awards.

If the norm bonus percentage rises with increasing salary, is this not another case of the rich getting richer?

On the surface, it would surely seem so. However, there used to be two good reasons for the practice, and today there is still one good one.

Not so very long ago, the U.S. had a highly progressive tax structure. Until 1964, for example, it was possible to find yourself in a 91 percent marginal tax bracket, such that only $0.09 of each additional dollar of income ended up in your pocket. With a tax structure that steep, it became imperative to offer higher bonus percentages at the top of the organization if only to assure that senior executives received about the same percentage increase in after-tax pay as those in more junior bonus-eligible positions.

Now, however, the maximum tax rate has been lowered to 50 percent. Moreover, this 50 percent marginal rate cuts in at a fairly low level of compensation, such that most, if not quite all, bonus eligibles would be at the maximum rate on the basis of their salary alone. Therefore, the argument that higher and higher bonus percentages are needed to offset higher and higher tax rates is simply no longer valid.

But the second argument is still very much alive. This argument speaks to the concept of risk and reward. Assume here that a survey of the comparator group shows that the going rate of salary-plus-short-term-incentive-award (hereafter called Total Current Compensation—or TCC) for the CEO is $600,000 per year and that the going rate of TCC for the most junior bonus-eligible position is $60,000. Assume further that your company decides to structure its arrangements in the following manner:

- The CEO will be assigned to a salary grade containing a midpoint of $375,000. In addition, he or she will be granted a norm bonus equal to 60 percent of salary.

- The junior executive will be assigned to a salary grade containing a midpoint of $50,000. In addition, he or she will be granted a norm bonus equal to 20 percent of salary.

On the basis of the above, each executive will receive a competitive level of TCC, assuming that each is performing acceptably and assuming further that the company is performing acceptably. Now see what happens under other assumptions:

- Assume first that the company has a disaster, such that no executive receives any bonus that year. In that case, the actual TCC of the CEO will be $375,000 versus a norm level of $600,000. In effect, he is now earning only 62.5 percent of competitive TCC. The junior executive, on the other hand, will earn 83.3 percent of competitive TCC. In this case, therefore, the decline in TCC for the junior executive was less than it was for the CEO. Accordingly, because of the nature of its incentive compensation arrangements, the company implicitly exposed the junior executive to less compensation risk than it did the CEO.

- Now assume that the company has a marvelous year, such that both executives receive twice their norm awards. In that case, the CEO will receive $375,000 of salary and $450,000 of bonus, for a TCC level of $825,000. In turn, this TCC level will be 37.5 percent higher than the competitive TCC level. The junior executive, on the other hand, will receive a base salary of $50,000 and a bonus of $20,000, for a TCC level of $70,000. In this case, he or she will be earning not 37.5 percent more than a competitive TCC level, but only 16.7 percent more.

  You can see here that although the junior executive is exposed to less risk than the CEO in a downturn, he also is exposed to less reward in an upturn. So there is a certain fairness here and not the injustice that is seemingly the case.

Can a company with lower-than-average norm bonuses be considered chintzy?

Not necessarily. The company may well take up the slack by paying substantially above-average salaries. The converse may be true in the case of the company that offers super-sized bonuses. Executive salaries in the auto industry, until very recently, were lower than those offered by other industries. But bonus awards could be huge, thereby more than offsetting the competitive salary decrement in even an average year.

From that perspective, therefore, you may decide you're better off in a company that offers a small bonus opportunity and a commensurately larger base salary. In such a case, your downside risk may be quite a bit less compared to the person in the company with a smaller base salary and a comparably larger bonus opportunity. Yet your upside reward may not be all that much smaller.

Which brings up a terribly important point. If you're considering changing employers, you simply cannot focus on only one element of the new employer's compensation package. Rather, you must look at all elements together and then construct some what-if scenarios to identify the circumstances under which your total compensation package would soar like an eagle or plummet like a stone.

If my norm award is equal to 30 percent of my salary, what will my maximum award be?

In general, a company will permit an award to rise to around 150 percent to 200 percent of the norm award level. Thus, if your norm award is equal to 30 percent of your salary, you might, if the moon and all the planets line up right, receive an award of 45 percent of your salary or, in some companies, as much as 60 percent of your salary.

If my norm award is equal to 30 percent of my salary, what will my minimum award be?

Your minimum award can be zero if everything goes wrong. From a practical standpoint, however, most companies are reluctant to eliminate an award entirely. Hence, if bonus funds are available and if you are not about to be fired, then you can probably expect to receive not much less than about half your norm award.

How does my company decide how much it will spend on bonuses for all eligible employees?

Most companies' short-term incentive plans are governed by a shareholder-approved funding formula. If you check back through several past proxy statements, you can generally find this formula mentioned. Or, if your employer is open-minded, simply ask for a copy of the legal text of the plan.

There are all sorts of different formulas in use, but most of them are fairly common in concept. That is to say, the bonus fund consists of some portion of the profits that is in excess of some minimum profit level. In turn, the minimum profit level is usually defined in relation to shareholders' equity or, alternatively, a combination of shareholders' equity and debt.

To illustrate, consider a formula that calls for the bonus fund to be equal to 5 percent of the pretax profits in excess of a 16 percent pretax return on beginning shareholders' equity. Let us assume here that shareholders' equity as of the beginning of the year is $100 million.

The first thing we know is that there will be no fund available unless pretax profits are greater than $16 million, which itself represents a 16 percent pretax return on beginning equity. Next, we know that for each additional $1 million of profit beyond $16 million, $50,000 will be thrown into the incentive fund. Hence, if profits rise to $26 million, thereby creating a funding corridor of $10 million, the total bonus fund will be $500,000. We also know that if profits doubled, from $26 million to $52 million, the bonus fund would rise from $500,000 to $1.8 million.

Note here how the incentive fund is leveraged. In our example, the $52 million pretax profit figure was double the $26 million initial figure, but the $1.8 million bonus fund was 3.6 times the $500,000 initial fund. Hence, we know that as profits rise, the bonus fund under this formula will rise at an even faster rate.

By the same token, as profits fall, the bonus fund under this formula will fall at an even faster rate. To illustrate, assume here that pretax profits last year were $52 million and that this year they dropped to $26 million. Hence, we have a 50 percent decrease in profits. But the bonus fund, which moves from $1.8 million to $500,000, drops by 72 percent.

If the company does not earn a level of profitability equal to its threshold, is it all over for executives that year?

Not necessarily. A number of companies have a so-called carryforward feature. This permits them to salt away any bonus funds from an earlier year that were not actually spent. Thus, if the bonus fund this year was $1.8 million, and if the company spent only $1.5 million on bonuses, then, assuming the company had a carryforward feature, the sum of $300,000 would be available to spend in some future year when the bonus fund that year was either nonexistent or pitifully low.

Do all bonus formulas incent pretax profits?

No. Some formulas are predicated on after-tax profits. In the first case, the company means to hold executives harmless from changes in tax laws—laws that they arguably can't control.

In the second case, the company argues that there are many uncontrollable elements in managing a business, and taxes is only one of them. To be sure, you may not be able to change the tax laws, but if you feel their effects, you will be more nimble in taking corrective action, like raising prices, for example. At the same time, not all changes in tax laws result in a reduction in profits. The investment tax credit, for example, is a case where eliminating the effects of taxes might also cause you to decide not to build a new plant, which, though it offers a relatively poor return on a pretax basis, offers a handsome return on an after-tax basis.

Do all bonus formulas incent return on equity?

Again the answer is no. A number of companies believe that basing an incentive fund on return on equity offers too strong a temptation for top management to leverage the company, taking on huge amounts of debt and hoping that times will not turn bad in some future year. These more conservative companies typically predicate bonus funds on what is known as *return on capital employed.* Capital employed is the sum of shareholders' equity and long-term debt having a maturity of more than one year. From that perspective, therefore, capital employed represents all the permanent capital in the business. If you have to earn a return on such capital, the argument goes, then you will be indifferent as to whether additional capital comes in the form of extra equity or extra debt.

The problem is that debt generates interest charges, which in turn lower profits, while equity does not. So unless the profit figures are recalculated, executives are decidedly not indifferent to the difference between equity and debt. Accordingly, companies using this approach add back to profits any long-term debt interest charges that had previously been deducted from profits. To illustrate, assume that a company has $100 million of equity and $30 million of long-term debt. Hence, its capital employed will be $130 million. Assume also that the company is paying 10 percent interest on the long-term debt, or $3 million per year. If its reported pretax profits for the year are, say, $30 million, its pretax profits for purposes of determining the incentive fund will be $33 million, or the sum of the reported $30 million and the $3 million of interest that had already been reflected in the $30 million figure.

Now the executive is truly indifferent to the difference between equity and debt. Both types of capital enter the denominator of the return-on-capital-employed fraction. And neither type of capital is permitted to cause a lowering of pretax profits through interest charges.

Unfortunately, however, in the process of making the executive indifferent to either taking on additional equity or additional debt, the company has made him indifferent to the costs of money as well. Looking back at the above example, what difference does it make if the $30 million of long-term debt carries interest of 10 percent or 20 percent? Whatever the interest, it will automatically be excluded in the computation of profits for incentive plan purposes. Consequently, if a potential new project, which will require another $50 million in debt, can earn a pretax return greater than the threshold return built into the incentive plan, why not go ahead with it, even though interest rates may be so high as to cause the project to be a total loser? To illustrate, assume that the company's funding formula calls for the incentive fund to be equal to 7 percent of all pretax profits in excess of a 12 percent return on capital employed. On that basis, extra funds will go into the incentive pool so long as a project earns more than 12 percent on its capital. Now assume that a potential new project is slated to return 15 percent on its capital before interest charges. That being the case, by borrowing $50 million and earning 15 percent on it, the bonus fund will be credited with an extra $105,000. (Here, the project has earned three percentage points more than the threshold rate of 12 percent. Hence, the profits in excess of the threshold rate will be $50 million × 3 percent, or $1.5 million. In turn, 7 percent of any extra funds are contributed to the incentive pool; 7 percent of $1.5 million yields $105,000.) And this $105,000 will be credited to the incentive pool no matter what the interest rate is on the $50 million of extra debt. If the interest rate turned out to be 18 percent, one would think the shareholders would want to administer a savage beating to management for borrowing at 18 percent and earning 15 percent than to give it $105,000 of extra bonus monies.

If a company's incentive plan does not have a carryforward feature, will the company spend all the funds generated each year?

You would certainly think so. After all, if you have no carryforward feature, that means any funds you don't spend will be lost forever. (At least, they will be lost to the executives. The shareholders, however, will reap greater profits because of the lowered costs.) But, in fact, it is frequently the case that a company with no carryforward feature in its incentive plan nonetheless does not spend the entire fund generated under the plan.

The reason lies in part in the leveraged nature of incentive funds, as just discussed. If profits boom to too high a level, the funds generated by the bonus formula could be so huge as to create an embarrassment on the proxy statement, if not an outright lawsuit, were they to be spent.

In addition, also consider that as a company grows, the number of executives eligible to participate in the incentive plan grows more slowly. After all, if the company doubles in size, it still needs only one CEO, one chief financial officer, etc. Hence, there is a tendency for funding formulas to become too lush over time.

You might think that if the funding formula is too lush, a simple way to fix it would be to ask the shareholders to reduce it. After all, would they ever refuse? The problem here, however, lies in the one-sided nature of shareholder relations. If you cut your funding formula, you are not likely to be carried out of the room on the shareholders' shoulders. But if you try to increase your formula later, you may be carried out of the room, period. That being the case, most managements are naturally slow to suggest that their incentive funding formulas be brought into synch with reality. In practice, therefore, many companies do not spend all the funds they could on bonuses in a year of excellent performance. However, as performance begins to decline, the percentage of the incentive fund that is actually spent typically starts to rise. In this manner, the company implicitly offsets, in whole or in part, the leveraged nature of the plan.

To illustrate, take our earlier funding formula, which generates a fund equal to 5 percent of the pretax profits in excess of a 16 percent return on beginning shareholders' equity. Assume first that the company earns $52 million of profits, thereby generating a $1.8 million fund. Now assume that instead of spending the entire fund, the company spends only $1 million, or 56 percent of the fund.

Finally, assume that next year profits decline from $52 million to $42 million. In this case, the fund declines from $1.8 million to $1.3 million. But note that the company need not make a proportionate decline in its bonus payments. Indeed, if it possesses sufficient perversity, it could confound everyone—executives included—and increase its bonus fund by 30 percent—from $1 million to $1.3 million. Although it probably won't go that far, it may well opt for only the most cosmetic of decreases—say, from $1 million to $950,000.

Note here that the company spent 56 percent of the funds generated by its formula in year 1 but a much higher 73 percent of the funds generated by its formula in year 2 (assuming the fund in year 2 is $950,000). Thus, you can see that by increasing or decreasing the actual expenditure percentage, the company can begin to subvert the original intention of the formula, which was to insure that funds for bonuses increase at a faster rate than profits when profits are rising and that funds for bonuses decrease at a faster rate than profits when profits are falling. In our example, profits declined by 19 percent, while bonuses declined by only 5 percent.

Are all bonus plans gutty?

Heavens no! The one we just looked at is a perfect example, since the company is managing the plan to cause bonuses to swing hardly at all in relation to profits. Indeed, some plans are so soft that they are nothing more than additional base salary in drag. So don't assume that your bonus will automatically be quite volatile. You may find that you can count on it to a considerable degree.

If I work in a division of my company, will my bonus be impacted by the performance of my division?

Most companies claim to take divisional performance into account in establishing bonus funds for their various profit centers. Whether they actually do, however, is another matter.

In many cases, the CEO uses discretion in allocating chunks of the overall corporate bonus fund to various divisions. For example, assume that the overall fund is $5 million and that that fund would be sufficient to grant each eligible executive an award equal to 110 percent of his or her norm award. At this point, the CEO looks at the performance contributions of each division and then determines the norm award percentage that he will give to each one. He may, for example, think highly of the contributions of Division A and therefore give it a fund equal to 140 percent of its norm awards. If he does, of course, he will have to recover the excess from some other division, since we are playing a zero-sum game here.

So, using his discretion, the CEO could, theoretically, vary norm award percentages all over the map and thereby send out all sorts of important messages to his troops in the field. However, the record at most companies suggests that the more discretion the CEO has, the less discretion he will actually use. Hence, don't be surprised to find that when the overall corporate fund is sufficient to grant all eligible executives an award equal to 110 percent of norm, each division receives a fund that is exactly equal to 110 percent of its norm awards—or, if not exactly equal, then terribly close to being equal.

The reason for this lack of guttiness stems, we think, from the fact that the use of discretion requires the person using the discretion to take personal responsibility for his or her acts. Hence, in slicing the funds for a given division, the CEO can't hide behind some formula. Rather, he has to admit that he, and he alone, did the terrible deed.

Your CEO may sound like the Wizard of Oz, but when you go behind all that fire-breathing apparatus, you are apt to find a human being just like yourself—a person who, when you get right down to that proverbial bottom line, wants to be loved.

Often you hear a CEO say that he'd rather fire someone than cut his or her bonus. In our view, this statement translates into the belief that "If you're going to hate me, it's better that you hate me at a distance, rather than from the next office!" So, though there may be smoke aplenty, there may not be all that much performance discrimination in bonus distribution.

Do all companies simply use discretion in determining funds for my division?

No. Some companies set up formulas to govern the funds a division will receive. One quite popular approach is to base the division's fund on how well it does in relation to its profit budget. Thus, division executives may be told that if they make budget, they will receive an award fund equal to 100 percent of their norm awards. They may also be told that for each one point increase or decrease over budget, their award fund will vary by two points. For example, if they make 110 percent of budget, then the fund will be 120 percent of norm awards; or if they make 90 percent of budget, the fund will be 80 percent of norm awards.

Basing bonus funds on making budget is a dangerous business. For one thing, it politicizes the budget-setting process to an even greater degree than would be the case were no incentive funds linked to budget. And everyone knows that there's politics galore in budget setting under the best of circumstances. At the same time, divisional executives are, understandably, quite leery about going way over budget. To do so obviously shows the top corporate executives that they are either poor business forecasters—or liars.

What is worse are the perverse incentive effects. If you budget for a disaster and then make it, you can be showered with rewards. But if you budget for a triumph and fall short, you can get the back of the corporate hand. So after a while, you learn to submit the lowest budgets you can get away with. And then you make sure that if you come in above budget, you don't come in very far above budget.

All of this does not mean, however, that there aren't intelligent formulas that can be used to determine divisional bonus funds; rather, basing bonus funds on achieving budget is not one of them—at least in most cases.

What's the advantage of using a divisional funding formula?

There are at least two advantages. First, the do-a-good-job-and-I'll-see attitude that lies at the heart of the discretionary approach is avoided. Rather, divisional executives know, and at the beginning of the year, just what they have to accomplish to earn a decent incentive fund. Thus, they can focus their efforts to maximize their earnings, and, if the right goals have been established, there's certainly nothing wrong with that. Second, a magnificently performing division is apt to receive a much larger fund than would have been the case under the discretionary approach, where the magnificently performing division would implicitly end up subsidizing its less successful siblings.

If there is a formula governing the funds for my division, does this mean that my award won't be impacted by overall corporate results?

Not necessarily. Few companies place all the emphasis on divisional performance. Rather, they place part of the emphasis on divisional results and part on corporate results. As a consequence, your division's fund is likely to be impacted to at least some degree by corporate performance.

Suppose my division does a great job, but the corporation does so badly that there are no funds in the overall incentive fund. What happens?

You are probably out of luck! If a company has no carryforward provision in its overall funding formula, then a corporate disaster is likely to mean a disaster for everyone, even including the one division that did its usual fine job.

If there is a carryforward feature, then you may get at least a few cents on the dollar. But you probably won't get the full fund to which you would otherwise be entitled, because all sorts of people will feel they have a right to share in the meager funds available from the bonus reserve. One of them is even likely to be your own CEO—the person whom the shareholders might reasonably indict as the principal guilty party.

Once in a while, however, you run into a truly independent divisional funding formula. In such a case, the division executives are guaranteed payment of all funds generated by the formula, notwithstanding that the corporation is actually losing money. The only exception would involve the corporation's entering Chapter XI.

Two companies I have worked with serve to illustrate the diversity of bonus approaches. Both of them have multiple divisions, and both operate in a series of disparate industries.

The first company has an overall corporate funding formula that covers all eligible employees in the company. And it also uses discretion in determining the funds each division will receive. The result is that great divisions rarely receive significantly more funds than poor divisions. And the corporate staff is also assured of a healthy slice of whatever fund is produced.

The second company's corporate funding formula covers only the corporate staff. And because the corporate staff can't appropriate other people's money in poor times, bonus payments to the corporate staff can be quite volatile. Then each division has its own separate funding formula—one that is guaranteed to be immune from corporate performance. In this second company, bonus awards to divisional executives vary greatly. Within the past few years, several divisions received no awards at all; yet the head of the company's star division received a bonus in the seven figures.

How about my performance as an individual? Does that count?

It may to some degree. Most companies claim to take individual performance into account in determining bonus awards. Ostensibly, they look at how well you have performed against the objectives that were established for you at the beginning of the year.

However, leaving official policy aside, the fact is that individual performance usually doesn't count for all that much. To be sure, if you walk on water, you may qualify for a bit extra—say, 110 percent of norm when everyone else is receiving 100 percent of norm. And if you have done poorly you may receive a bit less—say, 90 percent of norm when everyone else is receiving 100 percent of norm. But neither the

Elysian fields nor the gas chamber is much in evidence in most companies' bonus plans.

At the same time, there are some companies that, as a matter of policy rather than practice, do not recognize individual performance. Hence, if a fund is sufficient to give everyone 120 percent of his or her norm award, then everyone gets precisely that.

Does the IRS care how much I am paid, so long as I pay all the taxes I owe?

In some cases, the answer is a surprising yes; normally, you would think that the IRS would be in there rooting for the executive as long as it gets its fair share. If you work for a publicly owned company or even if you work for a privately owned one and are not yourself a major shareholder, you can probably be paid virtually unlimited amounts of compensation without attracting the attention of the IRS. But if you work for a privately owned company and are yourself a substantial shareholder, you may be in for problems.

To illustrate why the IRS is concerned, assume that you own all the stock of your company, pay yourself a salary of $100,000 per year, and are about to close the year with $1 million of pretax profits after paying all costs save a bonus for yourself. If you decide not to give yourself a bonus, you will be reporting $1 million of taxable income to the IRS and will pay, say, $400,000 in taxes. That leaves $600,000 in after-tax income. Now let's go on to assume that you pay yourself a dividend consisting of the entire $600,000 of after-tax income. Your total pretax income for the year is therefore $700,000, consisting of your $100,000 salary and your $600,000 in dividends. Meanwhile, your company has been drained of its entire $1 million of pretax profits, with $400,000 going to the IRS and $600,000 going to you. The IRS, of course, will also receive some tax money from you. If we assume, purely for the sake of illustration, that all personal income is taxed at 50 percent, then you will pay the IRS an additional $350,000 on your $700,000 of income, giving it a grand total tax take of $750,000.

Alternatively, let's assume that you decide, at the last minute, to award yourself a bonus equal to the entire pretax profits of $1 million. In that case, you declare to the IRS that your taxable income is $0, and your company pays no tax at all. Meanwhile, you have taxable income, not of $700,000, but rather of $1.1 million. If we again assume that all personal income is taxed at 50 percent, your tax bill here will rise from $350,000 to $550,000. But the IRS, which would have received $750,000 under the first alternative, now ends up losing $200,000.

You can now see why the IRS concentrates its fire on major shareholders of privately owned companies. Those executives well understand that they want to report the lowest corporate income possible and to pay themselves as much compensation as possible. And the IRS well understands that the way to governmental fiscal health lies in being able to tax the same income twice—once as corporate profits and a second time when the after-tax residue is declared as dividends.

Consider also the fact that when extra compensation is paid to an executive of a publicly owned company or one who works in a privately owned company and is not a major shareholder, the IRS usually ends up a net gainer. Had the compensation not been paid, corporate income would have been higher and the extra income would be taxed at a maximum rate of 46 percent. But when extra bonuses are paid, the IRS, although losing 46 percent from the corporate side of the tax equation, typically gains 50 percent from the executive. Hence, it usually comes out four points ahead in these situations.

I keep hearing about "caps" in various incentive plans. What does the term mean?

A cap refers to the fact that an incentive plan will reward performance only up to a certain point; beyond that point, extra performance generates no extra reward.

To illustrate, an executive might be offered an arrangement whereby he is to receive 5 percent of all profits in his division, but in no event more than 100 percent of his salary. Assume here that his salary is $150,000 per year. On that basis, we can determine that he will receive a bonus of $150,000 when the profits are $3 million per year. And we can also determine that he will receive not one cent more if the profits rise above $3 million per year.

Isn't the use of a cap rather demotivational?

It sure seems that way to us. If we can agree that something is worth incenting, then why is it not the case that more of that something should bring more pay?

What is often happening here is that the company is fearful of paying an individual too much money—even for the best of reasons. So it acts to limit the incentive effects of its incentive plan—something akin to shooting itself in the foot. Sad to say, but it sometimes seems that caps are used in incentive plans more than they are used in orthodontia!

Will my bonus be paid in cash—and right away?

In most cases. However, some companies insist on deferring part or all of your bonus. One approach involves paying you some portion of the bonus right away and then paying the remainder over the next few years. Thus, you may get 20 percent of the bonus right away and then receive an additional 20 percent each year for the next four years. A second approach involves deferring part or all of your bonus until your retirement.

What is meant by the term "golden handcuffs"?

A company that forces you to defer part or all of your bonus is likely to add insult to injury and require that you remain with the company as a condition to receiving whatever bonus has not yet been paid. Hence, if you quit before receiving a certain portion of your bonus, you will forfeit it entirely.

The golden handcuffs approach is often euphemistically described as an incentive to stay with the company. In reality, that is hogwash; the approach is nothing more than a disincentive to leave the company. It is negative in its approach, and it is negatively perceived by almost everyone on whom it is imposed.

Instead of forcing me to defer my bonus, how about simply letting me decide whether or not I want to defer?

A large and growing number of companies will do just that. Indeed, they may give you quite a bit of flexibility. For example, if you have a child entering college in eight years, you may be able to defer for eight years and then have the deferred amount paid out over the following four years. Or, if you wish, you may defer all the way to retirement and then have your deferred monies paid out in anywhere from, say, five to fifteen annual installments.

But if you are going to be given a choice, the company must take precautions to insure that you won't run afoul of the IRS's Doctrine of Constructive Receipt.

What is the doctrine of constructive receipt?

If you could claim that you received income whenever you chose to receive it, one wouldn't get very good odds betting against your deciding to defer its receipt for as many years as you could get away with. Hence, the IRS has ruled that you must recognize income for tax purposes the first time you can reach out your hand and take it, even though you do not choose to reach out your hand. This doctrine explains, for example, why you are taxed on the annual interest credited to your savings account, even though you do not withdraw the interest; after all, you could have withdrawn the interest, had you chosen to do so.

So, if you've already worked the entire year and then try to defer your bonus, the IRS, although happy to let you defer it, will have its hand out for the current tax liability. That, of course, would represent the worst of both worlds.

To get around this problem, companies permit you to elect to defer a bonus at only certain times. For example, a highly conservative company may require you to make a deferral election prior even to the beginning of the fiscal year for which the bonus will be earned. Thus, if your bonus for 1985 performance is normally paid in March 1986, you will have to make a deferral election on or before January 1, 1985, if you want to defer your bonus. On the other hand, some companies permit an election to be made during the year for which the bonus will be paid, but usually not during the last quarter of the year.

If you know that you want to defer, it is always best to file your election as early as possible and not to wait until the last minute. That way, you will be minimizing the possibility of the IRS nabbing you under its Doctrine of Constructive Receipt.

So, if I defer, I gather from the above that I won't have to pay any tax until I later receive the money. Is that right?

You got it!

If I am permitted to decide whether I defer, and if I do decide to defer, will I lose the money if I later decide to quit the company?

Crazily enough, there are some companies that will try to pull that one on you. I guess they figure you may be stupid enough to go for it. To be sure, you might be absolutely resolute in your desire to stay with your company; therefore, those golden handcuffs provisions have no meaning for you. But don't forget that the fine print also says that you will lose your money if the company fires you. And although you might successfully contest a discharge and regain your deferred funds, you can look forward to a long court battle and a lot of legal fees.

If I defer, is the company going to pay me some interest?

If the company doesn't offer you some sort of return on your investment, you need a psychiatrist, not an investment counselor, should you decide to defer. After all, your money will simply erode in value. Most companies do offer you some sort of return. In most cases, the return consists of crediting your deferred account with interest. But in other cases, the company's stock is used as the deferral vehicle. And in still other cases, the company invests the money in a diversified portfolio.

What sort of interest will I receive?

Most companies will credit you with interest at the prime rate. In a few other cases, the interest rate may be a bit lower or higher. For example, one company offers the same interest rate as savings bank pay on certificates of deposit, while another company offers the prime rate plus four points.

So I get the prime rate. Big deal! If I'm at the 50 percent tax bracket and the prime rate is 12 percent, I will only be earning 6 percent after-tax interest. Right?

Wrong! Assume that you defer a $10,000 bonus for ten years, with the prime rate being 12 percent in each future year. On that basis, a compounded interest rate of 12 percent will cause the $10,000 to increase to $31,058 at the end of ten years.

When you receive your deferral check for $31,058, you will be required to pay a tax at ordinary rates on the full amount. So, assuming you are in the 50 percent tax bracket, your tax will be $15,529, and you will be left with $15,529.

As an alternative, assume that you decided not to defer but rather to take the $10,000 bonus in cash at the time it was first earned. Assuming here that you were again in the 50 percent tax bracket, you would have paid $5000 of taxes and been left with an equal $5000 amount.

Suppose you went down to your local broker and invested the $5000 in municipal bonds carrying 12 percent interest. And suppose further that every time you received an interest payment on the bonds, you reinvested the interest in more bonds, with the new bonds again carrying 12 percent interest. On that basis, your tax-free funds would grow from $5000 to $15,529 at the end of ten years. And that is the same $15,529 you earned from the deferral!

Hence, we can state a firm mathematical rule here. Assuming that your tax rate later will be the same as it is now, then whatever interest rate you earn during the deferral period will be an after-tax rate of interest as far as you are concerned.

On that basis, a 12 percent after-tax interest rate may not look too shabby, given that you probably can't find an equivalent rate in the outside world without taking on more risk—and perhaps a lot more risk.

Speaking of risk, could I ever lose the monies in my deferred account?

Even though there are no golden handcuffs provisions in your deferral agreement, you could still lose your entire principal (and any interest that had accrued) if your company goes belly up. In such a case, you would become a general creditor of the company and would have to stand in line with the other creditors to receive your money. In all probability, you might only receive a few cents on the dollar. In the case of most companies, however, the risk of bankruptcy is, happily, quite low.

How about a deferral in my company's stock?

If you defer your $10,000 bonus in company stock and if the company's stock is then selling for $50 per share, you will be credited with 200 shares. Then, when the deferral period is over, you will either be delivered certificates for 200 shares or else be paid a cash amount equal to the then value of 200 shares.

If dividends are declared during the deferral period, the company may elect to pay them to you right away or, alternatively, to defer them. Paying dividends right away is sort of nutty, given that by deferring you signaled your desire not to have any further current income. Moreover, you end up paying a tax on the dividends as soon as you receive them. If the dividends are deferred, as is usually the case, some companies credit the dividend amount in cash and then credit you in future years with interest at whatever the rate applicable to cash deferrals. Thus, company performance may impact the dividend itself, but once the dividend is declared, company performance has no further impact.

The more usual approach, however, is to let your dividends earn more dividends by being converted into additional company shares. Assume here, for example, that you deferred $10,000 in the form of 200 company shares. Then, a few months later, the company declares a dividend of $1 per share, or $200 on all 200 of your shares. Assuming the then market price of the company's stock is $55 per share, you will be credited with an additional 3.64 shares ($200/$55). Hence, you will now have 203.64 shares in your deferred stock account.

Assume further that one quarter later, another dividend is declared, but this time it is a higher $1.10 per share. This dividend will then be applied to your 203.64 shares, rather than to your original 200 shares. Hence, you will start to earn dividends on dividends.

Of course, you will continue to have your deferred funds impacted by future company performance. If performance is poor, the dividend may be cut, and, worse, the stock price may fall, thereby reducing the value of all your deferred shares.

If I defer in company shares, what will my tax treatment be when I receive the shares?

You will not be eligible for capital gains tax treatment, since you were never the owner of record of the shares during the deferral period. Instead, in the year you first receive the shares, you will be taxed at ordinary rates on the value of the shares at the time you receive them. For example, if you receive 250 shares in 1989 with a then value of $100 per share, you will have to pay tax at ordinary rates on $25,000. In turn, your cost basis in the shares will be increased to $25,000; thereafter, you will be treated as an ordinary investor. Hence, if you later sell the shares for $30,000, you will have a $5000 capital gain; and if you later sell the shares for $20,000, you will have a $5000 capital loss.

Whether that gain or loss will be a long-term capital gain or loss, or a short-term one depends on whether you have held the shares for six months or more after first receiving them. Note here that the time the shares were held in the deferral account does not count in determining whether you qualify for a long-term capital gain or loss transaction.

How about an investment in a diversified portfolio?

A while back, we indicated that some companies offer this sort of investment. Typically, deferred funds are managed by outside investment experts, and there may even be more than a single fund offered. For example, you may get to choose between a high-risk equity fund and a low-risk bond fund. In this sort of situation, you will almost invariably receive cash at the end of the deferral period, rather than the underlying securities. And you will be taxed at that time on all the cash you receive.

From your standpoint, a diversified portfolio may represent an ideal deferral medium. However, that may not be the case from the company's standpoint, due to the fact that dividends and gains on securities other than the company's own stock are taxable to the company. So you won't find this sort of investment medium offered very often. But if you do, consider it carefully, because it may be ideal for you.

Don't deferrals make even more sense given that I will be in a lower tax bracket after retirement?

They would if your given turns out to be correct. To be sure, you will be receiving less income after you retire than when you were an active employee. But because of normal pay raises and promotions between now and the year you retire, as well as the effects of income tax bracket creep, your pension income may well be sufficient to leave you in the same 50 percent tax bracket you were in just prior to retirement. Nonetheless, a deferral may still make economic sense even if your analyses show that you won't be in a lower tax bracket when you retire than you are in now.

You seem pretty bullish on deferring income. Isn't there any downside to deferring?

Sorry if you got that impression. There certainly is a downside. First, when you make an election to defer, that election becomes irrevocable. So if you decide to defer your bonus until your retirement, then you can't decide five years from now (which is, say, ten years before your retirement) that you want to be paid your deferred monies. (Any deferral agreement that gave you the ability to call for the money when you wanted it would represent an instant violation of the IRS's Doctrine of Constructive Receipt.)

So, one disadvantage of a deferral is a loss of liquidity. We also talked earlier about the possibility that you might lose the deferred income in the event your company went bankrupt. So there's a second disadvantage, although the probability of it materializing is low.

You may also find, in retrospect, that the investment media used for deferrals were not very good. Suppose, for example, that your deferred monies are invested in company stock and that the company stock plummets. Hindsight being what it is, you will surely have known to sell the stock just before it started its descent. But you couldn't sell it because the terms of your deferral agreement didn't offer you any other investment choice. Or perhaps other choices are available, but you are permitted to revise your investment elections only once a year. That being the case, you may miss the prime time to sell or buy. So a third potential disadvantage of deferring compensation is a loss of investment flexibility.

Finally, you may be banking on your income tax rate at the time you receive deferred income being lower than it was when you made the decision to defer—or at least the same. But changes in intervening tax laws may work to cause your tax rate at the time of deferred income receipt to be higher than it was at the time you originally deferred. In that case, your assumption that deferrals would save you tax dollars turned out to be utterly worthless.

You can see, therefore, that deferring income is not always the right decision. Nonetheless, if you have some spare cash, you ought to analyze carefully what your company is offering and see if that offer represents a potentially better deal than you could get by investing on your own.

SECTION THREE

LONG-TERM INCENTIVES

Appropriately, this lengthiest section of the book is devoted to long-term incentives. Not too many years ago, an executive's pay package consisted of a base salary, an opportunity to earn a bonus based on annual performance, perhaps a perk or two, and the usual broad-based fringe benefit programs (retirement, life, medical, etc.).

Then a new form of executive compensation began to emerge. Its basic purpose was to make executives think more like owners who were concerned not only with maximizing income right this minute, but also with insuring the company's long-term success. These new long-term incentives consisted at first of stock option grants. But as time passed, companies began to adopt many different forms of long-term incentive compensation.

At the same time, the size of long-term incentive grants, and their potential value, began to increase. Today, it is not uncommon for the value of long-term incentive grants, under fairly vanilla future performance estimates, to exceed the value of annual bonus opportunities. And, if you are in a senior-enough position, it is not uncommon for the value of long-term incentive grants, again under the same fairly vanilla future performance estimates, to exceed the value of your entire base salary. So we now have a potent and potentially huge form of additional executive compensation.

In looking over the long-term incentive landscape, did you know that:

- New tax laws permit you to purchase option stock and have the entire appreciation in the stock's value treated as a long-term capital gain.

- You can receive a stock option carrying an option price that is lower than the fair market value per share of your company's common stock on the date of option grant.

- If you are a so-called corporate "insider" (usually an officer or director of the parent company), ways can be found to deliver your option profits in cash so that you never need worry about having to return profits to the SEC and/or to incur downside risk during a six-month holding period.

- You don't necessarily have to pay cash to exercise your stock option shares. Many companies now permit you to use shares of company stock you already own.

- Even though your company's long-term performance plan offers increasing payouts only for increasing EPS growth, you can still receive a handsome payout even though the EPS in the last year of the long-term performance period is lower than the EPS in the year prior to the start of the performance period.

- Quite a few companies are willing to give you totally free shares. To earn them, it is not necessary for the company to achieve any particular level of performance during the next few years. Rather, all that is required is that you remain with the company for a period of time.

- Some companies are now offering what is known as *junior stock*. Here, you can purchase company shares at a fraction of their current market price (as little as 10 percent) and yet convert all future gain into a long-term capital gain.

- The payouts you receive under your company's long-term incentive compensation plans are apt to bear no relationship to whether your division performed well during the past few years—or abysmally.

- Your personal performance contributions are unlikely to impact either the payouts you receive under your company's long-term incentive plans or the size of your future long-term incentive grants.

What's a long-term incentive plan?

There is a bewildering variety of long-term incentives offered by various companies, but they all have one thing in common: They are intended to reward you for performance accomplishments over a period of several years, rather than for just a single year.

Why have a long-term incentive plan?

You might think that an intelligently designed short-term incentive plan is incentive enough. After all, if the plan offers an unlimited incentive, you will be out there trying to maximize the company's earnings and thereby help the shareholders.

That's just the trouble—you may well be trying to maximize the earnings. But some of the ways you choose could threaten the company's future viability. For example, you can always give a quick rise to profits by cutting down, or eliminating, the R&D budget. Or by cutting back on product quality in ways that don't show up for several years. Or by eliminating management development. Or by not maintaining equipment. Or by not investing in new and more productive equipment. The ways are almost legion, but each of them has the effect of hyping up current earnings and probably contributing to the company's eventual demise.

If that demise happens, of course, you will pay the price by seeing your short-term incentive award cut to zero. You might be fired on top of that. But all this can happen only if you are still with the company. Alternatively, if you milk the earnings and then depart just before the company falls apart, you will not only not pay a penalty but will also gain the reputation of being a miracle worker. (When Joe was running the place, the profits were awesome. Now Joe's left, and the profits have gone to hell.) Accordingly, by offering you not only a short-term incentive award opportunity but also the opportunity to earn even more if long-term performance is good, your temptation to maximize current earnings at the expense of long-term viability will, theoretically, be eliminated.

What's the most popular long-term incentive around?

The stock option. It comes in two types: The nonqualified stock option (NQSO) and the incentive stock option (ISO).

What's a nonqualified stock option?

Some years ago, the Congress permitted companies to offer a stock option that carried favorable tax status. The Congress called it a qualified stock option. To obtain the favorable tax status, however, the option had to meet certain requirements, some of which could be considered onerous under various circumstances. In addition, the company could lose its tax deduction on the implicit compensation it was giving the executive.

As a result, some companies decided to offer different types of stock options. Although these different options were not all alike, they did share one attribute in common: They were designed in a manner that did not permit them to be considered as qualified stock options. The people who designed these second types of options didn't call in some Madison Avenue firm to dream up some fancy name. They simply called them nonqualified stock options.

There's an irony here in that Congress, in 1976, killed off the qualified stock option. But its opposite, the NQSO, still lives, even though its name is no longer particularly meaningful. Indeed, it should now be called the nonincentive stock option.

An NQSO gives the optionee the right to purchase a fixed number of shares of company common stock over a fixed term for a fixed price.

How long an option term does an NQSO offer?

In almost all cases, you will have ten years from the date of grant of the option to exercise it.

What is the option price of an NQSO?

In almost all cases, the option price per share equals the fair market value per share (FMV) of the company's stock on the date of option grant. Thus, if you are to receive an option today, and the FMV of your company's stock today is $50 per share, then the option price will likely be $50 per share. You can see, therefore, that if the FMV rises above $50 per share during the next ten years, you stand to make some money.

In a few cases, the option price is lower than the current FMV of the stock. For example, one large company uses as its option price the book value per share at the end of the preceding year, not the FMV of the stock on the date of grant. Given that the market price is usually higher than the book value, the company is offering an implicit price discount compared to other companies.

May I exercise the option at any time during its term?

Generally not. Different companies impose different exercise restrictions. The most liberal companies may tell you that after waiting one year from the date of grant, you may exercise any of the shares in your grant during the remaining ten years. On the other hand, a more conservative company may tell you that you may only exercise 25 percent of the shares after waiting one year. Then after waiting two years, you may exercise 50 percent of the shares (less any shares you have exercised earlier). After waiting three years, the percentage rises to 75 percent. Finally, all exercise restrictions are removed four years from grant.

Do I have to exercise my grant all at once?

No. You usually have quite a bit of flexibility and can exercise it in as many bite-sized pieces as you wish. Of course, you can also exercise the entire grant at once if you want to.

How do I go about exercising my grant?

You pay the company a sum of money equal to the product of the number of shares you are about to exercise and the option price per share. When it receives the money, the company will deliver the certificates to you.

Do I have to pay a tax upon exercise of the grant?

Yes. The amount by which the aggregate FMV of the shares you have exercised exceeds your aggregate option price is considered as ordinary income to you in the year of exercise.

To illustrate, assume that you are exercising 200 shares of option stock at an option price of $50 per share. Hence, you pay the company $10,000. Assume further that the shares have a value of $75 each at the time of exercise. Hence, you have a paper profit of $25 per share, or $5000 on all 200 shares. It is this $5000 figure that you will have to take into your ordinary income.

When do I have to pay this tax?

Your company is required to make an immediate withholding. However, the withholding rate is likely to be no more than 20 percent of the paper gain. Hence, assuming you are in the 50 percent tax bracket, you may not have to ante up the remaining 30 percent until the April 15th following the end of the year in which you exercised the option. In some cases, however, you may have to file an estimated tax declaration and pay some or all of the remaining tax earlier.

Do I have to pay a further tax when I sell my NQSO shares?

That depends. Let us go back to the example just used, where you exercised 200 shares at an option price of $50 per share and at a time when the FMV was $75 per share. By paying $50 per share and then being taxed on the $25 per share gain, you have established a cost basis per share of $75.

If you subsequently sell the shares at $75 each, there will be no further tax to pay. However, if you sell the shares for more than $75 each, you will have a capital gain on the excess over $75. The gain will be a long-term one if you have held the shares for six months or more past their exercise; otherwise, the gain will be a short-term gain.

If you sell the shares for less than $75 each, you will have a capital loss equal to the difference between the actual sales price per share and $75. The loss will be a long-term capital loss if you have held the shares for six months or more past their exercise; otherwise, it will be a short-term capital loss.

What does the term "registered shares" mean?

It means that the shares have been registered with the SEC and may be freely sold after their exercise. On the other hand, if the shares are not registered, you will probably be required to certify that you are buying the shares for investment and not for resale. Although you can change your mind and subsequently sell the shares, you may be denied this privilege for up to two years.

Almost all companies register their shares. Those few that don't either are trying to save a few bucks (the SEC imposes registration fees) or else are using nonregistration as a means of making you hold on to your shares. Before you exercise a stock option, always determine whether the shares are registered.

What does the term "insider" mean?

The term stems from Section 16(b) of the Securities Exchange Act of 1934. That act, among other things, tried to stem the abuses that were then prevalent on the part of people who had inside knowledge of company affairs and could thereby reap windfall profits. Under the law, officers and directors of a company were deemed to be insiders.

An insider who buys company stock and then sells it at a profit within six months must return the profits to the company. Similarly, an insider who sells company stock and then buys it at a profit (i.e., a lower price) within six months must also return the profits to the company.

Hence, an insider is not going to execute a buy–sell or sell–buy transaction within a six-month period, unless there is no profit. And that is the purpose of the law.

They call me a vice-president. Does that mean I am automatically an insider?

Not necessarily. Some companies are open-handed with officer titles, but from a strictly legal standpoint, many of the officers are not considered to be true officers of the company. This is true of many banks and advertising agencies, for example.

One key as to whether or not you will be considered an officer for purposes of the SEC insider-trading regulations may lie in whether you are an elected officer or an appointed officer. At some companies, for example, senior officers are elected by the board of directors, while other officers are appointed by the CEO, with no board approval required. From a legal standpoint, these appointed officers are not considered officers at all. Although they may be disappointed to learn this, they can at least console themselves with the fact that, unlike the true officers, they can buy and sell company stock at will. If you are a true insider, your company will doubtless let you know about it.

If I don't have an officer's title, does that mean I can never be considered an insider?

You can never be considered an insider under Section 16(b) of the Securities Exchange Act. But you can be considered an insider under Section 10(b)(5) of that same Act. This section applies to anyone who has inside information other than those covered by Section 16(b) of the Act. However, there is no set time period during which you must hold the shares or else forfeit the profit. Rather, you are free to sell your shares the minute your inside information is no longer considered to be inside information, that is, it is in the hands of the general public.

As an insider, what are my tax consequences on an NQSO?

You will not incur a tax liability on the exercise of the option. Instead, you will first incur a tax liability when the insider trading period has expired (i.e., six months after exercise) and the shares can be freely sold. Thereafter, you are treated just like any other optionee, as just described.

To get around the insider trading provisions, may I exercise my option stock and then sell some other company shares I own?

No! The SEC has promulgated its doctrine of fungibility in this regard. Hence, shares are shares, and it doesn't matter that you are selling physically different certificates.

As an insider, what happens if my shares rise in value during the six-month holding period?

Any increase in value ends up being taxed as ordinary income, notwithstanding that you subsequently hold the shares long enough to qualify for a long-term capital gains tax advantage. To illustrate, assume the following: You exercise 200 shares at $50 per share when the FMV is then $75 per share. The FMV goes on to rise to $90 per share by the end of the six-month holding period. You continue to hold the shares for another twelve months, by which time the FMV has risen to $100 per share.

In that case, you incur no tax during the six-month holding period, and then you incur a tax on $40 per share, or on $8000 for all 200 shares. The tax will be levied at ordinary rates. Then, when you sell the shares, you will be taxed at long-term capital gains rates on the $10 per-share appreciation ($2000 in all) that occurred during the twelve months prior to sale.

As an insider, what happens if my shares fall in value during the six-month holding period?

Once again, you will incur no tax liability during the six-month holding period. At the end of the period, you will take into your ordinary income the amount, if any, by which the current value of the shares exceeds what you paid for them. To illustrate, assume again that you have exercised 200 shares at $50 per share when the current FMV is $75 per share. In this case, however, the FMV drops to $60 per share by the end of the six-month holding period. At this point, you will take into your income the sum of $10 per share, or $2000 for all 200 shares. Taxes will be levied at ordinary rates, and you will have then established a new cost basis in the shares of $60 apiece.

As an insider, can I end up losing not only the gain that existed at the time I · exercised the option shares but also some or all of my original investment?

Only if you let yourself. Note that there is nothing to prevent you from selling your shares during the six-month holding period if there has been no gain.

Hence, if you exercise your shares at $50 apiece, it might be prudent for you to call your broker and place a stop-loss order at $50 per share. In that case, if the shares do lose all of their gain, you can still recover the amount you paid for them (less brokerage fees, of course— and also the interest you might have paid on the funds required for exercise).

If I have an NQSO that has not expired and my employment is terminated, what happens?

If you resign voluntarily and without the company's consent, you may be permitted to exercise your option only during a ninety-day period following your termination (but not beyond the normal expiration date of your option, if earlier than ninety days after termination). However, a growing number of companies require you to forfeit the option immediately upon termination. (Although you lose the opportunity for any further risk-free appreciation beyond termination, you can, of course, exercise the option just before handing in your resignation.)

A discharge is generally handled like a voluntary resignation. If you should become disabled or die, you (or, in the case of death, your estate) are typically permitted to exercise the shares during a one-year period following termination (but again, not beyond the normal expiration date).

Finally, if you should retire under your company's retirement plan or if you should resign with the company's consent, you may be permitted to exercise your option shares during a significantly longer period. In many companies, you would be permitted to exercise your shares within a three-year period following termination (but again, not beyond the normal expiration date). In a few companies, the period is even longer—up to five years. And in a few other companies, it is shorter—down to only ninety days.

Do I have to pay cash when I exercise my stock options?

In the past, the answer was almost invariably yes. But in recent years, an IRS ruling has permitted you to use stock you already own. In the trade, this is known as a stock-for-stock exercise.

Here's how it works. Let's assume that you have an option on 1000 shares at an option price of $50 per share. The stock has risen to $80 per share, and you feel it is time to exercise. As it turns out, you already own another 1500 shares, which you obtained through an earlier NQSO exercise. With regard to that earlier exercise, the option price was $20 per share and the FMV at the time of exercise was $35 per share. Hence, your cost basis in the 1500 shares you already own is $35 per share.

At this point, you hand back to the company 625 of the 1500 shares you already own in payment for the 1000 option shares you now wish to exercise. Since the 625 currently owned shares have the same value as the price you must pay to exercise the option ($50,000), the company turns around and issues you the 1000 option shares.

Let's pause here for a moment. You turned in 625 currently owned shares and received 1000 option shares. Thus, you started with 1500 shares and ended up with 1875 shares (1500 original shares less 625 shares turned in plus 1000 option shares received).

Under this transaction, the IRS considers that you made a tax-free exchange of 625 shares you then owned for 625 of the 1000 option shares you acquired. Hence, on those shares, you continue to carry your original cost basis of $35 per share. But the IRS also considers that you received the remaining 375 option shares free. Since they are worth $80 each, and you have been considered to have paid nothing for them, you must take into your income their total value of 375 × $80, or $30,000.

There you have it. You started the transaction owning 1500 shares with a cost basis of $35 per share. And you ended the transaction owning 1875 shares, 1500 of which carry a cost basis of $35 per share and 375 of which carry a cost basis of $80 per share. In addition, you had to take into your ordinary income the sum of $30,000.

Is there really any advantage to me to use company shares to exercise my stock option rather than to pay cash?

There's nothing all that earthshaking about the new-found ability to use company shares to exercise a stock option. However, the use of shares can certainly help you with your financing problems. Assume that such an alternative does not exist and that you have to come up with $50,000 in cash to exercise your 1000 option shares. As you know, you already own 1500 shares of company stock with a cost basis of $35 each. You also know that for each share you sell, you will have to pay a long-term capital gains tax. The tax will consist of 20 percent of the amount by which the current $80 FMV exceeds your $35 cost basis. Hence, the tax will be ($80−$35)×20 percent, or $9. Your proceeds per share will thus be $71, and you will have to sell 705 shares to raise the $50,000 you require. (In fact, you will have to sell more shares than that because of the need to pay brokerage fees.) You make this sale and then use the proceeds to purchase your 1000 option shares. As already mentioned, you also take $30,000 into your income and pay a tax on it.

Remember that, under a stock-for-stock exercise, you ended up with 1875 shares and a tax liability on $30,000. Now, you end up with

1795 shares and the same tax liability of $30,000. You can see the advantage of a stock-for-stock exercise. By taking this route, you get to delay the taxes you would have to pay were you to sell some of your currently owned shares at the time of exercise. You don't, of course, avoid those taxes entirely, because when the shares are finally sold, the tax will then be due.

Does every stock option plan contain a stock-for-stock exercise provision?

No. Among other things, the company must receive the approval of its shareholders before implementing such a provision. Nevertheless, a growing number of companies are introducing the stock-for-stock exercise provision into their option plans.

If I don't already own enough shares with which to make a stock-for-stock exercise, may I make a partial option exercise and then turn around and use my newly acquired option shares to make a second stock-for-stock exercise?

In many cases, yes. Indeed, if you think about it, you could adopt a true pyramid approach by buying a single share on the open market, turning it in to the company in a partial exercise, taking the newly acquired option shares and turning them in for another partial exercise, and so on until the entire option was finally exercised.

A number of companies do not permit this type of pyramiding, however. It is not that they see anything immoral about the act; rather, their accountants have told them that permitting pyramiding may expose them to severe charges to earnings.

In this regard, some companies require that any stock turned in for exchange must have been held by the executive for at least one year (or, alternatively, for at least six months).

If the FMV drops substantially below my option price, will the company consider reducing the option price to give me a second chance to reap some gain?

Sometimes. Technically, the company probably cannot lower your option price. But what it can do (assuming it has the shareholders' approval for this type of action) is to cancel your existing option shares and to reissue you new option shares at an option price that is equal to today's lower FMV. The company must have your permission to do so, however, but one would think the permission would be forthcoming in something less than four nanoseconds.

Option swaps, as these actions are called, are frequently denounced by shareholders. Consider, for example, the hapless shareholder who buys some shares at $50, watches the price first drop to $20 and then rise to $40, and finally sells the shares at $40. He has sustained a loss of $10 per share. On the other hand, his counterpart inside the company receives some option shares at $50, watches the price first drop to $20, obtains an option swap with the new option price at $20, and then exercises the shares when the stock moves back up to $40. Here, the executive has reaped a $20 profit per share at the same time the shareholder was losing $10 per share.

Because of this, many companies are understandably leery about granting an option swap. If they do, it is likely to be accompanied by some form of penalty. For example, if you now own 1000 shares with an option price of $50 per share, you may receive in exchange for those shares only 600 shares with an option price of $20 per share. Or the term of the new option shares may extend only to the time the former option shares would have expired.

INCENTIVE
STOCK OPTIONS

What is an incentive stock option (ISO)?

Since 1950 the government has offered favorable tax treatment to certain types of executive stock options, provided the options contained certain characteristics. If you have been granted an ISO, your company will let you know about it.

What will be the option price of my ISO?

By law, the option price per share must not be less than the FMV per share on the date of grant. It can be higher, but that is hardly ever likely to be the case.

How long will I have to exercise my ISO?

The law permits a maximum term of ten years. However, some companies utilize a lesser term, typically five years.

What happens if my employment is terminated?

Practice is generally as described previously for NQSO's, but with one exception. By law, you may not, except in the case of death, be permitted to exercise your option beyond a period of ninety days following termination (or, if earlier, the option's normal expiration date).

This limiting provision is often not noticed by an executive. Obviously, it may make little difference to someone who is remaining with the company. But if you are going to quit or retire, it can make a lot of difference.

May I exercise my various stock options in any order I choose?

No. You can exercise in any order if you have an NQSO, but this is not the case with an ISO. The law provides that you must exercise your options in the order they were granted.

From a practical standpoint, this means little if the FMV of your company's stock always rises. This is because each later option will carry a higher option price; that being the case, you wouldn't want to exercise the options except in the order they were granted.

But suppose you received one option for 1000 shares at $50 per share and a later one for 1000 shares at $30 per share. Then the FMV recovered to $40 per share. In such a case, you could not exercise your second option (which contains a paper profit of $10,000) before first exercising your first option (which contains a paper loss of $10,000).

This so-called order-of-exercise provision is a nasty sleeper in an ISO grant. It can effectively deny you a lot of profit and for a lot of years if things go wrong.

If I'm blocked from exercising an ISO, how about cancelling the earlier grant?

The IRS is one step ahead of you here. As it turns out, it is easier to kill Count Dracula than it is to kill an ISO. The IRS says that an ISO that is cancelled stays alive for the purposes of the order of exercise provision. Hence, cancelling an earlier ISO grant represents the worst of both worlds; you lose the possibility of making some money on that grant in the future (after all, the stock price may recover smartly); and it doesn't help you a bit in attempting to get at a juicy ISO granted at a later date.

What if my second option grant is not an ISO grant but an NQSO grant?

No problem. The order-of-exercise provision applies only to a subsequent ISO grant. Hence, you can exercise the NQSO anytime it is exerciseable by its terms. Because this is so, a company that grants ISOs may well decide to make its next grant an NQSO in the event that the FMV has fallen sharply since the last ISO grant was made.

Do I have some sort of tax obligation when I exercise an ISO?

Not under normal circumstances. However, if you have a lot of tax-sheltered income, it is possible that you could end up paying a tax of 20 percent on part or all of the amount by which the aggregate FMV of the stock on the date of ISO exercise exceeds the aggregate exercise price. This is because such amount is considered tax preference income for purposes of computing the so-called alternative minimum tax.

Note that the alternative tax is just that—an alternative tax. From a practical standpoint, it does not come on top of your regular taxes; rather, it replaces them, and only if it is higher.

Note also that paying this alternative minimum tax does nothing to change the cost basis of your shares. Hence, if you end up paying this tax, it will be a new tax and will not cause the regular tax consequences associated with an ISO to be any lower than they would have been without this tax.

In most circumstances, of course, executives have a lot of income, and most of it remains unsheltered. Thus, it is unlikely that you will ever run afoul of this alternative minimum tax. But it is good to remember that it exists, because if it does look likely to cut in, you could at least consider delaying your ISO exercise until a future year when you have a more normal tax liability.

Does this mean that if I can avoid the alternative minimum tax, I will pay no tax whatsoever in conjunction with my ISO exercise?

Yes. That is one of the substantial advantages of an ISO grant as compared to a NQSO grant.

What happens when I sell my ISO shares?

That depends. If the date of sale is at least two years after your ISO shares were granted and at least one year after they were exercised, then you qualify for long-term capital gains tax treatment on the entire amount by which the then aggregate FMV exceeds your aggregate exercise price. By the same token, if you sold the shares at a loss, you would have a long-term capital loss.

To illustrate, assume you exercise an Incentive Stock Option on 1000 shares at an option price of $50. The FMV at grant is $75, and one year later when you sell the shares the FMV is $100. Assuming that you escape the Alternative Minimum Tax, you end up paying no tax on exercise of the ISO. And when you sell the shares, the entire $50,000 gain is taxed as a long-term capital gain.

However, if you do not meet the above holding requirements, you will be deemed to have made what is known as a disqualifying disposition. In that case, you will end up paying tax at ordinary rates. The tax will be levied on your entire gain, that is, the amount by which the aggregate FMV at exercise exceeds the aggregate exercise price.

As you can see, an ISO offers an attractive tax advantage, if it is held long enough to qualify. Instead of paying a maximum tax of 50 percent on your paper gain when you exercise the option, you end up paying a maximum tax of 20 percent on your actual gain, and then only when you sell the stock.

Note, however, that if you get stuck with the Alternative Minimum Tax, you could end up paying a total tax as high as 40 percent. Assume, for example, that your ISO paper gain is $100,000 at the time of exercise. Under all the wrong circumstances, this entire $100,000 could attract a $20,000 tax under the Alternative Minimum Tax rules. Go on to assume that after holding the stock for one year, you sell it at the same price as it was worth on its exercise. Thus, your actual gain will be $100,000. Assuming you are at the maximum 50 percent tax bracket for ordinary income, your long-term capital gains tax rate will be 20 percent, and you will end up paying another $20,000 to the government. Hence, your total tax was 40 percent of your gain, rather than the expected 20 percent.

As indicated several times, it is rather unlikely that you will encounter the 20 percent Alternative Minimum Tax, either on the paper gain at exercise or the actual gain at sale. But knowing that such taxes are possible will help you avoid having to pay them. Remember that by simply moving your exercise to the next tax year, you may be able to avoid all or most of the effects of the Alternative Minimum Tax.

If ISOs are so good, why not grant only ISOs and forget about granting further NQSOs?

For all their tax advantages, ISOs have a number of problems. First, as mentioned earlier, there is a potentially nasty order-of-exercise provision. Second, as also mentioned earlier, an ISO cannot be exercised for very long after termination of employment, except in the case of death. Third, the price the company pays to get you long-term capital gains tax treatment is the loss of its own corporate tax deduction. Because this is so, an ISO transaction can rarely be considered cost-effective for the company.

To illustrate, assume that the company grants you 1000 NQSO shares at an option price of $50 per share and that you exercise the shares at a time when the FMV is $75 per share. You pay the company $50,000, and the company issues you 1000 shares. Then the company deducts your paper gain of $25,000 ($25 per share × 1000 shares) on its own income tax return. Since the company is most likely at a 46 percent marginal tax rate, the result is that its taxes are lowered by 46 percent of $25,000, or $11,500. Hence, the total proceeds the company receives from the transaction are not merely $50,000 but a higher $61,500.

If the company wished, it could enter the open market and buy in as many shares as it could for its $61,500 of incremental cash. Given that the price of the shares is then $75 each, it could buy in 820 shares. And since it issued you 1000 shares, the net effect would be to reduce the net share issuance from 1000 shares to 180 shares. This 180-share figure represents the true cost of the transaction to the company, since it implicitly issued those 180 shares for no consideration whatsoever, all the remaining considerations having been used to repurchase the 820 shares.

Now assume that instead of being granted 1000 NQSO shares, you are granted 1000 ISO shares. Given all the above assumptions, the company will receive net exercise proceeds of only $50,000; this is because it cannot deduct the $25,000 paper gain on its own income tax return. Hence, it can repurchase only 667 shares with its proceeds, instead of the 820 shares as was the case with the NQSO transaction. That means that it has issued, for no consideration whatsoever, 333 shares instead of 180 shares.

So although it is true that you can save taxes through an ISO transaction, it is also true that the company's costs are higher. And because the company is losing $0.46 of tax relief on each dollar of ISO gain at the same time you are gaining only $0.30 of tax relief (the difference between the maximum 50 percent tax rate for ordinary income and the maximum 20 percent tax rate for a long-term capital gain), the transaction is decidedly not cost-effective. Indeed, the real winner here is neither you nor the company, but rather the IRS. The IRS ends up making $0.16 on each dollar of gain, compared to an NQSO transaction.

A fourth disadvantage of an ISO is the fact that the number of shares that may be granted is limited by law. (There is no legal limit imposed on an NQSO grant.) According to the law, you may not receive a grant in any one year the size of which is more than $100,000, unless you have received a lesser grant in some earlier year. By size, we mean the product of the number of option shares to be granted and the option price per share. Hence, if the FMV at the time of grant is $50, you may not receive a regular grant of more than 2000 shares.

In the event that your grant in any one year is less than $100,000 in size, half the difference—but only half—may be carried forward for use during one or more of the ensuing three years. So if your employer gives you only $50,000 of ISOs this year, another $25,000 can be carried forward to another year. But the other half of the foregone grant, that is, $25,000, is lost forever as far as a further ISO grant is concerned. It is for this reason that most companies using ISOs make grants every year rather than at more infrequent intervals.

You should also consider that if you exercise an ISO and go for the favorable tax treatment, you will have to take on some downside risk during the holding period. Thus, if the stock starts to drop in value, you will have to decide whether to abort your try so as to minimize the loss or else to grit your teeth and hang on to the end of the holding period, hoping that the stock will recover—or at least stop its decline. Remember that if you abort your try and sell the stock short of the one-year holding period, any gain that you realize will be taxed at ordinary rates and not at long-term capital gains rates.

Moreover, you will have to incur some interest costs, or some opportunity costs, during the holding period. This is because the dividend yield on the stock, even calculated off your favorable purchase price, may not be sufficient to cover the interest costs you may have incurred to borrow the funds necessary for exercise.

Wait a minute! Let me understand something. You say that the government makes money on an ISO grant compared to an NQSO grant. Yet you also say that the government limits the size of an ISO grant compared to an NQSO grant. How can that be?

Beats me! When you think about it, if the government reasons like this, we could end up running a deficit in this country.

STOCK APPRECIATION RIGHTS

What is a stock appreciation right?

A Stock Appreciation Right (SAR) permits you to take out the gain in a stock option without having to make any investment yourself.

To illustrate, let us go back to our earlier option transaction involving the grant of 1000 shares at an option price of $50. Assume that an SAR is attached to each option share and that the FMV rises to $75 per share. As you know, you can always exercise your option, paying the company $50,000 in the process. But now, with your SAR, you can elect to have the option cancelled and to instead receive an economic benefit equal to the paper gain of $25,000. This economic benefit could come in the form of $25,000 cash; or it could come in the form of 333 free shares of stock worth $24,975 (333 shares × $75 per share) and $25 in cash.

Who gets SARs?

In most companies, SARs are limited to insiders—those executives who, as discussed earlier, cannot make buy-sell or sell-buy transactions at a profit within six months without having to return the profit to the company. By using an SAR the insider may be able to sidestep, in whole or in part, the onerous holding requirements imposed by the SEC.

If I am an insider, how do I get cash for an SAR?

First, your company has to have an SAR provision that permits the settlement of an SAR in cash. Second, you have to apply for the cash payment. But you are not permitted to make your application anytime. Rather, you must apply during the period commencing with the third business day following release of your company's quarterly earnings statement and ending on the twelfth day following such release. And third, a committee composed of disinterested directors (i.e., those who cannot participate in the option plan—usually outside directors) must approve your application.

The reason for all the time restrictions is to minimize the possibility that you will be in substantial receipt of inside information at the time you exercise your SAR. By law, a company is required to tell its shareholders of any significant developments at the time it releases its quarterly earnings statement. That being the case, the SEC has reasoned that it takes about three business days for the information the company has released to become widely available (e.g., through the Dow Jones News Service).

Note again that you do not normally get the benefits of both an SAR and a stock option. When you exercise your SAR, your option shares are cancelled. And when you exercise an option, your SARs are cancelled.

If I am exercising an SAR for shares of stock, rather than for cash, do I have to observe the SEC rules regarding timing of application?

Generally not. The reason lies in the fact that the acquisition of shares under the exercise of an SAR for shares constitutes a buy under the SEC rules. You have been deemed to have bought the shares for $0 per share. That being the case, you cannot sell them under any circumstances for six months without having to return the profits to the company.

Well, that's not entirely true. If the shares plummet in value to $0 per share, you could sell them and have no gain to return to the shareholders. But then there wouldn't be any shareholders to return a gain to anyway, would there?

What are the tax consequences of an SAR exercise?

If you receive cash in settlement of an SAR exercise, you will take the entire cash amount into your ordinary income in the year in which you receive the payment.

If you receive stock in settlement of an SAR exercise, you will take the entire value of the shares received into your ordinary income in the year in which you receive them. The value in this case is measured by their value on the date of receipt. This value also becomes your cost basis should you later sell the shares. As mentioned earlier, if you hold the shares for six months or more before selling them, then any gain over your cost basis becomes a long-term capital gain, and any loss becomes a long-term capital loss. Otherwise, the gain or loss becomes a short-term gain or loss.

Why should SARs be limited to insiders?

There are two reasons that most companies would offer. The first is that the paper gain on most stock options is not charged against a company's reported earnings. To be sure, there is a cost to the option in that shares have to be issued, which in turn dilutes the earnings of the remaining shareholders. But the cost is relatively invisible.

In contrast, the payment of cash or shares under an SAR provision triggers a full charge against reported earnings. Moreover, the charge is potentially open-ended, since, at the time it first offered the SAR provision, the company did not know just how high the stock might climb. One way to limit this potentially high SAR earnings charge is to limit the number of executives to whom SARs are extended.

The second reason involves the fact that most noninsiders have what amounts to a do-it-yourself SAR kit. Provided the option shares are registered and can be freely sold, and provided further that there is no pressure on the executive to hold the shares after exercise, the noninsider can freely sell his or her shares as soon as he or she exercises them. Indeed, some companies have arrangements with outside firms to handle the disposition of option shares in a painless manner. The noninsider gives the outside firm a power of attorney. Then, when the executive wishes to exercise, he or she places a phone call to the outside firm. That firm, in turn, uses the power of attorney to exercise the option and advances the executive the required funds. The shares are then sold immediately and the proceeds (after deducting brokerage fees and a fee imposed by the outside firm) given to the executive. No fuss. No bother. And no charge to reported earnings, either.

On that basis, therefore, the grant of an SAR to an insider does not really confer an advantage vis-à-vis the noninsider; rather, it simply places the insider on the same basic footing as the noninsider.

Are there any other ways to control charges to earnings associated with an SAR transaction?

Yes, but none are very palatable. For example, some companies grant SARs to more executives than insiders. But they grant only one SAR for each two option shares granted. You can get partial relief, but not full relief.

Other companies take a different tack. For example, one company attaches an SAR to each option share and makes SAR grants to all optionees. However, the SAR cannot be exercised at all during such times when the FMV of the stock has advanced 50 percent or more over the option price.

Still other companies impose an outright cap. A common provision is that no more than 100 percent FMV appreciation may be recognized in the SAR. To illustrate, let us again go back to our 1000-share option grant with an option price of $50 per share. Assume that the stock rises in value to $110 per share. In such a case, the SAR feature would offer only the equivalent of $50 per share. By exercising the SAR, therefore, the executive would have his or her 1000 shares cancelled and would receive either $50,000 in cash or 454 free shares worth $49,940 (454 $\times$ $110) and $60 in cash. In effect, the executive would have lost the economic benefit represented by the difference between a share price of $100 per share and the actual share price of $110 per share. Of course, the executive could always obtain that extra benefit by foregoing the right to exercise the SAR and instead exercising the stock option.

Anyway you slice it, therefore, SARs present problems for the company and do not confer a truly great advantage, except to insiders.

If I can reach out my hand and take cash using an SAR transaction, why don't I have a constructive receipt problem?

From the standpoint of logic, you should have a problem. But the IRS has long agreed that if you must pay a significant penalty to reach out your hand and take income, then you will not be deemed to be in constructive receipt of the income until you actually do reach out your hand. The penalty in this case is the forfeiture of the related option grant, which usually has some time remaining before it is cancelled and which would always have some value if it could be sold to an outside investor. Hence, you should not experience any constructive receipt problems if your options come equipped with SARs.

Is an SAR really all that great?

Not really! An SAR, if its exercise triggers the cancellation of a related stock option, does not offer the executive an extra economic benefit.

Rather, it offers the same benefit in another form—a form that may be somewhat, but not always, more attractive. The important thing to remember is that if the FMV goes nowhere, then an SAR is worth precisely zero.

Indeed, is any stock option all that great?

Again, that depends on what happens to the FMV of your company's stock. If there is a huge movement, you can make lots of money from a stock option. But if there is no movement, you will make nothing.

It is sometimes the case that you will make nothing even though there is huge movement. This is because you don't exercise at the right time or because, after having exercised at the right time, you sell your stock at the wrong time.

In any event, however, stock options constitute a prime executive status symbol. In most circles, it is considered gauche to go to your country club and brag about your salary or bonus. But it is considered perfectly acceptable to bemoan the fact that your stock options are underwater (i.e., the then FMV is lower than your option price). This revelation is sure to get you a mixture of awe and sympathy. So even an underwater option can have at least some value.

How volatile are stock options?

The proper response to this question is, "Compared to what?" Shortly, we will be making a number of comparisons, but to set the stage, let's start with the stock option.

First, here are some key assumptions:

- Your company grants you 1000 NQSO shares at an option price of $50 per share. This also happens to be the FMV of the stock on the date of grant.
- EPS in the year preceding grant of the option were $5. Therefore, the price/earnings multiple of the stock was 10x at grant.
- Gain, if any, in the option is measured halfway through the ten-year term of the option, or after five years.
- EPS growth in future years is, alternatively, 0 percent, 5 percent, 10 percent, 15 percent, or 20 percent per year.

- The future price/earnings multiple is, alternatively, 10x (the same as it was at grant—we call this a *constant* P/E scenario); or 5x (a 50 percent decline compared to the P/E multiple at grant—we call this a *decelerating* P/E scenario); or 15x (a 50 percent increase compared to the P/E multiple at grant—we call this an *accelerating* P/E scenario).

To see what happens here, let us first look at what we will call the *central* scenario, that is, the one featuring the middle EPS growth assumption of 10 percent and the one featuring the middle P/E multiple assumption of 10x:

- Given 10 percent per year future EPS growth, EPS for the fifth year following grant will rise from $5 to $8.05.
- Given a constant P/E multiple of 10x, the FMV at the end of the fifth year following grant will be $8.05 × 10, or $80.50.
- Given an option price of $50 per share, the gain on exercise will be $80.50 − $50, or $30.50 per share.
- Finally, given a grant of 1000 shares, the aggregate gain on exercise will be $30.50 × 1000, or $30,500.

Of course, this particular gain of $30,500 will materialize only under the assumptions described and not under any of the other fourteen scenarios we tested.

The results of all fifteen scenarios can be seen in three graphic exhibits. Exhibit 7A first shows what happens to the five EPS growth scenarios when we assume in each case that the P/E multiple remains constant. Exhibit 7B shows what happens to the same five EPS growth scenarios, with each this time combined with a decelerating P/E multiple (i.e., 5x). Finally, Exhibit 7C again takes the same five EPS growth scenarios and combines them with an accelerating P/E multiple (i.e., 15x).

You can see from these exhibits that the gain can range from nothing all the way up to $136,600. Although these payout lines do not mean much at the moment, they will take on considerable meaning later, as we compare them to the payout lines that develop from using long-term incentive compensation devices other than pure stock options.

EXHIBIT 7A   Stock Option Grants (Value of Grant)

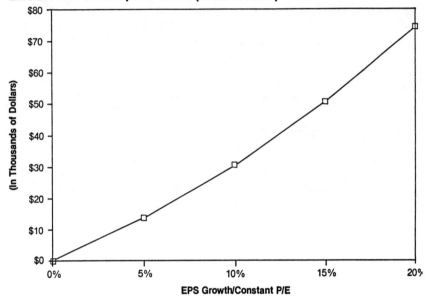

EPS Growth/Constant P/E

EXHIBIT 7B   Stock Option Grants (Value of Grant)

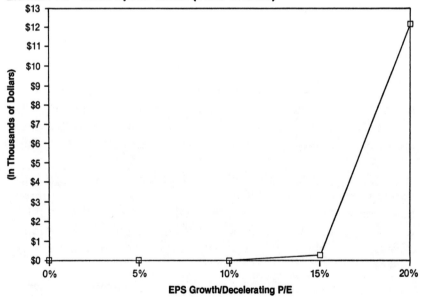

EPS Growth/Decelerating P/E

EXHIBIT 7C   Stock Option Grants (Value of Grant)

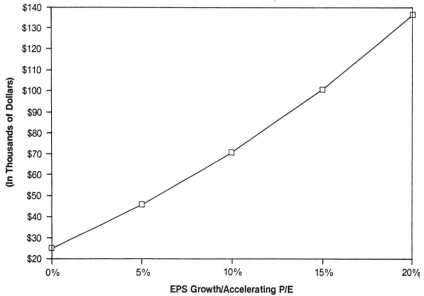

Who receives option grants?

Different companies have different eligibility criteria, but almost all companies restrict the grant of stock options to a smaller group than is the case with short-term incentives. Thus, if a company offers short-term incentive eligibility to those earning around $40,000, it may start offering option grants to those earning around $50,000.

How frequently are stock option grants made?

It depends on the company. Sometime ago, option grants were quite sporadic, often depending on the CEO's assessment as to whether the stock had hit bottom. However, in more recent years, most companies have adopted systematic granting frequencies.

The most popular frequency is annual. By making annual grants, a company can do a bit of dollar averaging with the option prices and thereby mitigate the risk of making a huge grant at a totally anomalous price. Second, the company has more flexibility in tailoring the size of

83

grant to individual performance circumstances. Third, offering grants every year gives the company a chance to say "I love you!" more often.

A close favorite alternative is to make grants every other year, in approximately twice the size as would be the case with companies making annual grants.

Finally, some companies seem to draw their timing out of tables of random numbers. No one really knows when the CEO is going to decide to recommend a new round of option grants—and the CEO is seemingly just as much in the dark as the rest of the executives.

How large will my grant be?

The most common approach to deciding your size of grant is to assign you a multiple of base salary. Thus, if your base salary is $100,000, you might be assigned a multiple of 1.0x, thereby entitling you to receive that number of shares having an aggregate option price of $100,000. Accordingly, if the option price is going to be $50, you receive a grant of 2000 shares. And if the option price is going to be $100, you receive a grant of 1000 shares. And if the option price is going to be $25, you receive a grant of 4000 shares.

The option multiple you are assigned is apt to increase with increasing salary, as shown in Exhibit 8, which shows general industry option multiples that have been annualized (i.e., sizes adjusted as if all companies made grants every year). Note that if your company makes grants at less than annual intervals, you would need to adjust these figures. For example, a typical granting multiple for a biennial grant would be 2.0x at the $100,000 base salary level.

You should also note that option multiples vary all over the map. In other words, if the average multiple at $100,000 of base salary is 1.0x, there will be some companies offering multiples as high as 3x to someone earning a base salary of $100,000, and other companies offering as low as 0.3x.

If the price of my stock rises, why do I get fewer shares and vice versa when the price drops? Shouldn't it be the other way around?

You would certainly think so. In general, the higher the price compared to the immediate past, the less appreciation potential there is. But many

EXHIBIT 8   Stock Option Grants (Typical Company Practice)

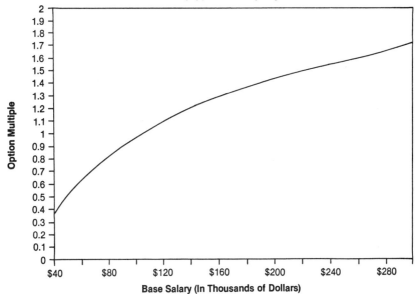

companies defend the practice on the basis of simplicity and not necessarily on the basis of logic.

Do option grants vary with either corporate or individual performance?

The possibility is certainly there, but few companies bother to make much distinction in the size of their grants. In essence, the option multiple schedule works the same in every year.

PHANTOM STOCK

What is phantom stock?

In general, a phantom stock grant is the same as an SAR grant, but without an underlying stock option grant and with the SAR having a fixed exercise date.

For example, your company might offer you 1000 phantom units at a time when the FMV per share of your company's stock was $50.

85

Then the company would promise you a payment five years from now, with the payment equal to the amount, if any, by which the FMV at that time exceeded $50 per share. Assuming that the FMV had increased from $50 to $75 per share, you would receive a check for $25,000. Or you just might receive a distribution of 333 shares, together with $25 in cash. Some companies offering phantom stock also offer dividend equivalents.

What's a dividend equivalent?

A dividend equivalent typically entitles you to receive a cash payment every time a dividend is declared, with the cash payment equal to the dividends payable on a single share of common stock.

Hence, if you received 1000 dividend equivalents to accompany your 1000 phantom units, and if the first dividend declared is $0.50 per share, you will receive a check for $500 at the time the dividend is paid to the shareholders.

What's the tax treatment of phantom stock and dividend equivalents?

It's all ordinary income. Whatever you receive is taxed at ordinary rates in the year you receive it. There is no capital gains tax advantage here.

Why have phantom stock?

In truth, few companies use phantom stock anymore, since an SAR offers a much more flexible transaction. With an SAR, you may be at the mercy of the FMV on the date of grant, but you can choose within very broad limits when you want to exercise. But with a phantom stock grant, you are at the mercy of the FMV on two dates—the date of grant and the date the grant is valued. It could prove to be the case that either of those two dates—or both of them—are faulty, thereby giving you nothing.

What are performance shares?

One of the major problems associated with stock options is the uncontrollable nature of the P/E multiple. Your CEO certainly has a significant degree of influence over the future EPS of your company. But the chairman of the Federal Reserve Board has far more influence over the P/E multiple of your stock than your chairman does.

Because the P/E multiple is so uncontrollable, it is sometimes the case that executives in a company granting stock options end up receiving nothing from their stock option grants, notwithstanding that the company's reported financial performance was excellent.

The purpose of performance shares, therefore, is to mitigate the influence of the P/E multiple on an executive's long-term incentive rewards and increase the influence of controllable, long-term company financial performance.

How does a performance share grant work?

In essence, an executive is promised x shares free, with the shares to be delivered at the end of a y-year performance period, provided the company achieves certain financial performance objectives. If the objectives are not fully met, the number of shares earned declines below x. And if financial performance is poor enough, the number of shares earned declines to zero.

To illustrate, let us describe one company's plan:

- The executive receives a grant of performance shares each year. The current grant is for 474 shares at a time when the FMV is then $50 per share.

- Financial performance is measured over a five-year period, starting with the year of grant.

- If EPS growth works out to 12 percent or more, the executive earns 100 percent of the contingently granted shares at the end of the five-year performance period.

- If EPS growth is equal to 10 percent per year, the executive earns 80 percent of the contingently granted shares at the end of the period.

- If EPS growth is equal to 5 percent per year, the executive earns 20 percent of the contingently granted shares at the end of the period.

- If EPS growth is less than 5 percent per year, the executive earns no shares at all.

Note that the company is now offering the executive a dual incentive. First, the number of shares the executive may earn is a function of long-term EPS growth. Second, the value of each share is still a function of the market price of the stock.

Let us first see what happens under the central scenario, which features 10 percent EPS growth and a constant P/E multiple of 10x:

- The executive earns 80 percent of the contingently granted performance shares. (It would have taken an EPS growth of 12 percent or more to earn 100 percent of the shares.) Hence, the number of shares earned is 379.

- The FMV has risen from $50 per share to $80.53 per share by the end of the five-year performance period.

- As a result, the value of the executive's shares are 379 × $80.53, or $30,521.

Now you can see why we chose such an exotic grant of 474 shares. We wanted to produce approximately the same $30,500 value under the central scenario as we produced with the 1000-share option grant.

However, just because both plans offer the same rewards under the central performance scenario, it does not follow that both plans offer the same rewards under all other performance scenarios. This can be seen in Exhibits 9A, 9B, and 9C, which contrast performance share and stock option plans under, respectively, constant P/E, decelerating P/E, and accelerating P/E scenarios.

If you first look at Exhibit 9A, you could easily conclude that a performance share plan is not very appealing. For poor performance, it delivers the same goose egg as a stock option grant. For normal performance, it delivers the same rewards. But for outstanding performance, it delivers materially less.

To an extent, that is actually the case with many companies' performance share plans. But the real value of such a plan lies in the fact

EXHIBIT 9A   Stock Options Versus Performance Shares

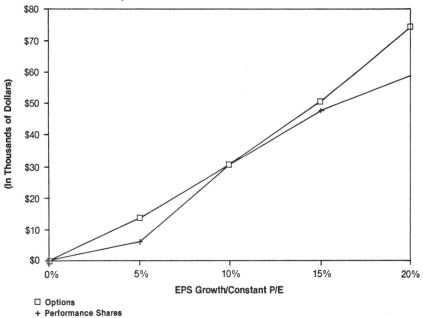

□ Options
+ Performance Shares

EXHIBIT 9B   Stock Options Versus Performance Shares

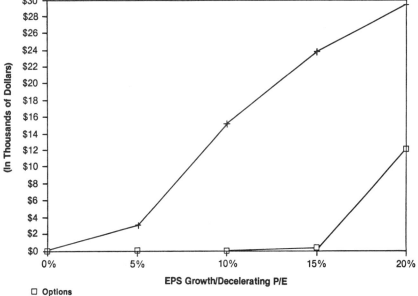

□ Options
+ Performance Shares

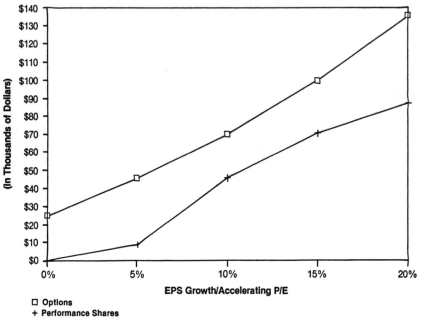

EPS Growth/Accelerating P/E

□ Options
+ Performance Shares

that internal financial performance might be magnificent at the very time when P/E multiples are plunging. For example, using the plan described, EPS growth might turn out to be 12 percent per year, but the P/E multiple of the stock also might drop in half, to 5x. With a 1000-share option, there would be no gain at the end of five years. But with a 474-share performance share grant, the executive would earn all 474 shares. And even though the market price would have declined from $50 to $40.26, the executive would still earn $19,083. This ability of performance share plans to stand up in the face of declining P/E multiples is shown in Exhibit 9B.

Of course, there is a *quid pro quo* here, and that is that performance shares do not yield gains as large as stock option shares when the P/E multiple is rising. Assuming company performance is sufficient for you to earn all 474 shares, you yield only $474 of additional income for each $1 gain in FMV, versus a much higher $1000 of additional income for each $1 increase in FMV in the case of stock options. The gap between the two types of plans is illustrated in Exhibit 9C.

90

Over what period of time is performance measured?

In theory, a company ought to choose a performance period length that matches the time it takes long-term decisions to come to fruition. So if you are a retailer, where about the longest decision to come to fruition involves deciding to build a new store, and if building a new store takes about three years, then a performance period length of three years would seem to make some sense. But if you are in the oil business, where it may take ten years to build a petrochemical complex, a ten-year period might make more sense.

To some degree, companies do take long-term decision time-frames into account in establishing the length of a performance period. But, in practice, almost all performance share plans feature performance period lengths of three, four, or five years—with four years being by far the most popular time period.

Assuming I am eligible, how often can I expect to receive a grant of performance shares?

Assume that you received your first grant of performance shares at the beginning of 1985 and that the performance period over which performance is to be measured includes the four years 1985 through 1988. That being the case, your next grant of performance shares is likely to be either at the beginning of 1986 or the beginning of 1987. If the grant is made at the beginning of 1986, the performance period for the second grant will cover the four years 1986 through 1989. Or, if the grant is made at the beginning of 1987, the performance period will cover the four years 1987 through 1990.

Hence, most companies make new grants of performance shares every year or every other year. Sometimes, however, a different pattern is used. For example, a company using a four-year performance period length might decide to make a new grant only once every four years. So if the first grant covers the four years 1985 through 1988, the second grant will cover the four years 1989 through 1992.

Am I missing something, or wouldn't I prefer to get a new grant of performance shares every year rather than every other year?

You're not missing a thing, assuming that the company would be willing to grant you the same number of shares in each grant, no matter whether grants were made annually or biennially. However, the company making the annual grants is very likely going to offer you half as many shares in a single grant as the company making biennial grants. So, over the long run, you may come out the same either way.

If there is no quantitative advantage to receiving grants every year, are there any qualitative advantages?

Yes, there generally are. First of all, smaller and more frequent grants offer the chance of dollar averaging the stock price. Second, because a new performance cycle starts every year, it is easier to add new executives to the plan. Third, performance targets can be changed faster, if a need to change performance targets arises. Fourth, since only half as many shares are riding on a single cycle, the downside for poor performance on a single cycle is not as great as is the case with biennial grants. Fifth, award sizes can be tailored to individual performance contributions, as well as your potential for advancement.

On the other hand, some people believe that making annual performance share grants may end up causing people to think that a performance share plan is just a second annual bonus plan. After all, if you receive a grant every year, with each grant featuring a four-year performance period length, then you end up receiving a payout every year, after an initial wait of four years.

That is certainly the case, assuming that future performance is always good. But if performance during one or more cycles is poor, then you won't be receiving a payout every year.

Some people also object to the fact that, with annual grants, each year of a performance period impacts four different performance share grants. Or at least that is the case once the plan has been up and rolling for four years. So if you have a terrible year, you may be regurgitating the terrible taste over four different performance cycles.

There's no denying the validity of the last point, but the alternative—starting a new performance cycle only every four years—creates more problems than it solves. Think about the fact that you have four times as many shares riding on what may turn out, in retrospect, to have been the wrong set of targets. Think about the problem of adding new executives to the plan. Think about the fact that, with all those shares riding on a single performance cycle, you just might be tempted to bring some revenues into the fourth year from the fifth year and to defer some costs from the fourth year to the fifth year. That would sure help your pocketbook, even if it might not help the poor shareholder.

What sort of tax am I going to pay on performance shares?

Assume that you are granted 1000 performance shares at a time when the fair market value of your company's stock is $50 per share. Also assume that at the end of the performance period, you earn all 1000 shares and that the fair market value of the stock has risen from $50 per share to $90 per share.

You will owe no tax at the time you are contingently granted the performance shares. This is because you were never actually granted the shares at that time; you only received a piece of paper indicating what you would actually receive four years later under certain circumstances.

However, when you actually receive the shares, you will have to take into your ordinary income the value of the shares you receive on the date you receive them. Hence, in our example, you will have to take into your ordinary income the sum of $90,000. Note here, though, that if the shares decline in value between the date of contingent grant and the date you actually receive them, then your tax will be less, too (just another example of the beneficence of our government!).

Do I have to pay the tax upon receipt of the shares even though I don't sell them?

Yes. The tax is due whether or not you sell the shares, the theory being that you were given property with an ascertainable economic value.

What happens if I hold the shares after receiving them?

By paying tax on the shares when you receive them, you establish a cost basis in the shares equal to the amount on which you are taxed. Thus, in our example, you received 1000 shares free, with each share having a then value of $90. And you paid taxes at ordinary rates on $90,000. Accordingly, your cost basis per share became $90.

Thereafter, you owe no further tax on the shares until you sell them. At the time of sale, any gain above your cost basis is taxed as a capital gain (a long-term gain if you have held the shares for more than six months after first receiving them; and a short-term gain if you have not). And any loss is taxed as a capital loss (long-term loss if you have held the shares for more than six months after first receiving them; and a short-term loss if you have not).

Do performance share plans require that all payouts be made in shares?

No, strange as that may seem. Quite a few companies, it turns out, deliver part of the economic benefit in shares and part in cash. Thus, if you earned 1000 shares and each has a then value of $90, the company might decide to deliver to you only 500 shares in certificate form, together with a check for $45,000. In that manner, you would have some liquid funds with which to pay all or a large part of your tax liability on the total economic benefit of $90,000. Indeed, some companies might even decide to forget all about the shares and simply pay you $90,000 in cash.

But if I get cash, how can they call it a performance share plan?

You've got a point there! However, don't confuse the payment medium with the incentive mechanism. If the company tells you that you can earn 1000 shares free depending on some future performance targets being met, you certainly have an incentive to do everything possible to improve your company's stock price, whether the company pays you in shares, in cash, or in coffee beans. After all, if the 1000 shares you earn are worth not $90 each at the end of the performance period but a whopping $180 each, then you will receive twice as much cash—or twice as many coffee beans.

If I am an insider and I receive shares, what happens?

Depending on the design of the plan, you may be deemed to have purchased the shares at a price of zero dollars per share. If that happens, then you won't be able to sell the shares for six months, since anything you receive for them exceeds what you paid for them.

However, it is possible for your company to qualify its plan as a bonus payable in shares. To illustrate the underlying logic, suppose the company decides to pay you cash in lieu of delivering performance share certificates, so it gives you a check for $90,000. In turn, you decide that you would really like to own some shares, so you ask the company whether you can buy shares with your $90,000 check. Being quite accommodating, the company agrees. You endorse the check and return it to the company. In turn you receive certificates for 1000 shares. You go home for the evening, pleased at having become what you believe is a substantial shareholder. But instead of gratitude from your spouse, you receive withering criticism for investing the family's hard-earned money in what your spouse believes is a poor investment. Besides, your spouse points out, where are you going to get the money to pay the taxes on the shares? Good point! The next morning, you race down to your broker on the way to work and sell the shares. Fortunately, the price is still $90 per share, so you are out only a small amount of brokerage fees.

Now, given all those circumstances, did you have an insider trading problem? Of course not. You bought the shares for $90 each and, although you sold them within six months of their purchase, you ended up receiving slightly less than $90 each.

That being the case, suppose that your company, instead of going to the trouble of issuing a check to you for $90,000, then having you endorse the check over to the company, and then handing you certificates for 1000 shares, simply handed you the certificates in the first place. Wouldn't you be in exactly the same position as in our example? And if that were the case, why should you have to return $90,000 of profits to the company if you decide, on your spouse's insistence, to sell the shares the next day?

The SEC conceded that this line of thought had something going for it—logic! So, it decreed that, under certain circumstances, a payment in shares would not constitute a purchase for purposes of the insider trading rules. Among the circumstances that must prevail is that you cannot be permitted to have a choice as to whether you will receive cash or shares; you must, by the rules of the plan, be given shares (or, if a choice is to be made, it must be made by a disinterested committee of outside directors). There are some other circumstances that also have to be met, but they are really not very onerous.

Suppose my shares do qualify as a bonus payable in shares. Am I home free as far as the insider trading rules are concerned?

Unhappily, no. To be sure, your acquisition of the shares did not constitute a purchase for purposes of the insider trading rules. But if you sell the shares, you sure do have a sale. Consider these facts: You receive 1000 shares having a then value of $90 per share, with the shares qualifying as a bonus payable in shares. You immediately sell the shares for $90 each. Then, with some of the proceeds from your share sale, you turn right around and exercise a stock option you received several years earlier. The option price is $50, and so you stand to make a quick profit of $40 per share.

Oh no, you don't. Note here that you sold shares at $90 and bought some other shares within six months at $40. Thus, you had a sale followed by a purchase in which there was a profit. Accordingly, you will have to disgorge the profits to the company. (The term disgorge is the SEC's very own. One wonders whether the person who drafted the insider trading rules was a gastroenterologist!)

So, even though a bonus payable in shares doesn't hang you with a purchase, you still have to watch your step during the six months after you sell those shares.

Suppose my receipt of shares doesn't qualify as a bonus payable in shares. As an insider, am I stuck with an immediate tax anyway?

Earlier, we said that you incurred a tax when you received a share distribution. But, to a degree, we lied. In fact, if you are prevented from selling the shares for six months because you are an insider, then you also delay your incidence of taxation until the end of the six-month holding period, that is, until the first time you can freely sell the shares. Then you are taxed at that time, whether or not you decide to sell the shares.

Note that the tax you pay is based on the value of the shares at the end of the six-month holding period, not at the time of initial receipt. If the shares rise in value, you will be paying taxes at ordinary rates on that appreciated value. (Had you not been an insider and had you held the shares for six months past their initial receipt, that appreciation would have been taxable at long-term capital gains rates.) But if the shares drop in value, you will avoid paying taxes on the amount by which the shares had depreciated.

Just who is eligible to receive performance shares?

Different organizations have different philosophies. But there are two basic patterns that can be observed. First, most companies extend eligibility for long-term incentive grants to fewer executives than the number participating in a short-term incentive program. And companies making performance share grants typically cover fewer executives than those making stock option grants.

When you strip away the romanticism, there aren't that many people in any organization who have a significant voice in making truly major decisions with long-term impact. To be sure, lots of people may get involved in staff studies, but they don't have the vote. In a company with, say, 10,000 employees, there may only be, say, twenty-five employees who are really long-term decision-makers. That number doesn't rise all that rapidly. Accordingly, in a company with, say, 100,000 employees, the number of long-term decision-makers may only rise to fifty.

Why are companies more liberal in extending eligibility for option grants than in extending eligibility for performance share grants?

First, performance shares seem more like real money than option shares. If the company does even reasonably well, you will get at least some of the shares. And they will be worth something, even though the market price may have declined during the performance measurement period. But with a stock option there is no guarantee of real money unless the stock price rises. And there is no guarantee of that even if the company's financial performance is fairly decent over the ensuing years.

Second, performance shares require charges to a company's earnings; most stock option grants do not. That, in turn, leads many top executives to think that stock option grants carry no cost. And if something carries no cost, why not be more generous?

Stock option grants do, of course, carry a cost, with the true cost being equal to the difference between what the stock is worth on the date the executive purchases it and what he or she pays for it. After all, if I sell you stock at $45 per share that I could have sold to the open market at the current price of $90 per share, any way you slice it, I have incurred a cost of $45 per share.

This is an example of the unintended incentive effects of accounting treatment. Under one type of plan, an executive can be given an economic benefit of say, $10,000, with the entire cost charged to earnings. Yet under another type of plan (a stock option plan), the executive can be given the same $10,000 economic benefit, with none of the cost charged to earnings. Sure, the costs of the second plan will show up in long-term dilution. But the costs take a long time to show up and will never show up as forcefully as charging $10,000 to earnings here and now. So, other things being equal, which plan would you choose if you were the person deciding for the company?

Fortunately, the illogic built into some of the regulations governing accounting for compensation plans involving stock is being seriously questioned from within the accounting profession. Indeed, a committee charged with examining the question recently recommended to the Financial Accounting Standards Board, the accounting profession's rule-making body, that all economic benefits from the exercise of stock option shares be charged to earnings, in exactly the same way charges to earnings are taken for stock appreciation rights.

So, one of these days, it may be possible for incentive plan designers to forget about accounting treatment and focus on developing plans that make economic and motivational sense.

Aren't performance shares worth more than option shares on a share-for-share basis? If so, doesn't that mean a company will grant fewer performance shares than option shares?

The answer to both of these questions is yes. Remember earlier we discovered that, under the assumptions being used, we could grant only 474 performance shares and yet generate the same economic benefit as 1000 option shares. Now 47.4 percent isn't always the precise trade-off ratio. But however you get there, a single performance share simply has to be worth more than a single option share. At least that is the case if performance is such that you earn it.

As a result, the typical company granting performance shares does indeed grant fewer shares to its executives than another company granting option shares.

When a company talks about performance in making performance share grants, what sort of performance does it mean?

In most cases, the company is trying to incent growth in earnings per share over a period of years. In some cases, however, goals are couched in terms of return on equity, return on capital employed, return on assets, and so forth.

How does the company go about measuring EPS growth?

To measure EPS growth, you first need a platform from which to start the measurement process, that is, a base-period EPS figure.

To illustrate, assume that a company earns $1 per share in the year preceding a performance share grant carrying a four-year performance measurement period. Assume too the following pattern of EPS during the four-year period:

EPS Performance Table

Year	EPS
1	$1.10
2	1.21
3	1.33
4	1.46
Total	$5.10

Most people don't realize it, but there are many ways to measure EPS growth. First, we could take the $1 base-period EPS figure and determine what rate of compounded annual growth would have to occur for four years to equal the $1.46 figure for year 4. The answer is, of course, 10 percent per year. This method of computing EPS growth is known as the *point-to-point method*. Note that we will get the same 10 percent-per-year answer as long as the base-period figure is $1 and the year 4 figure is $1.46, no matter what happens to the EPS in years 1, 2, and 3. For example, the company could lose $10 per share in year 2, instead of earning the $1.21 shown in the performance table, and yet it could still, with utter conviction, declare to its shareholders that it had increased its EPS at the rate of 10 percent per year during the four-year period under discussion.

The second method of measuring EPS growth consists of calculating the percentage increase in EPS in each of the four years and then averaging the four percentage figures so obtained. In the performance table shown, we would determine that each year's EPS is 10 percent greater than the EPS in the preceding year. Hence, the average EPS growth method would also yield a ten percent-per-year EPS growth figure. This method, as can be seen, doesn't let you get away with losing $10 in year 2, since the growth in EPS in year 2 over year 1 carries 25 percent of the weight in determining overall EPS growth during the four-year performance-measurement period. But percentages are notoriously difficult to work with. For example, suppose we had only a two-year performance-measurement period and that EPS were $1.50 in year 1 and $0.50 in year 2. In that case, we would record a 50 percent increase in EPS in year 1 over the $1 base-period EPS figure. And we would record a 66.667 percent drop in EPS in year 2 over year 1. Then, by averaging the two percentages, we would conclude that EPS had decreased at an 8.33 percent annual rate during the period. Unfortunately, we would also have to observe that the cumulative EPS of $2 earned during the period turned out to average $1 per year, or the same

EPS earned during the base period. On that basis, it would be hard to see how EPS had decreased 8.33 percent per year.

Or, consider the opposite situation, where EPS in year 1 decrease to $0.50, while in year 2 they increase to $1.50. Here, we record a 50 percent drop in EPS in year 1 compared to the base-period figure and a 200 percent increase in EPS in year 2 compared to year 1. By averaging the two figures, we now conclude that average annual EPS growth, far from being a negative 8.33 percent per year, is an astounding 75 percent per year. But we once again have earned an average of only $1 per year in each of the two years—the same amount as we earned during the base year.

A third method involves the use of regression analysis. We plot on the horizontal axis of a graph the years in which the EPS were earned, and then we plot on the vertical axis the related EPS figures themselves. A line of best fit is then drawn through the various dots on the graph. In developing this line of best fit, the EPS values are first transformed into logarithms. Because this is so, the slope of the resulting line of best fit yields a compounded EPS growth figure. This method, which is also called the log-linear method or the exponential method and is used most often by financial analysts in measuring EPS growth, takes into account the EPS experience of all five years (i.e., the base year and the four years in the performance-measurement period), rather than merely the base year and the last year. And it avoids the problems of averaging percentages, as just discussed. However, it too, has its pitfalls. Besides being complicated to explain, it often turns out that an anomalous EPS figure in either the base year or the last year will carry more weight in determining the slope of the line of best fit than will an anomalous EPS figure that is tucked somewhere in the middle.

Finally, we have the cumulative method of measuring EPS growth. The company first observes that the cumulative EPS during the four years in the performance-measurement period were $5.10 (per the EPS performance table). Then it asks itself this question: If we compound the $1 base period figure by X percent per year for four years and then add together the resulting four EPS figures (excluding the $1 base period figure itself), what will have to be the value of X so that the total of the four figures equals $5.10? The answer, once again, is 10 percent per year. Suppose, however, that instead of earning $1.46 in year 4, the company earned only $0.46. And suppose also that instead of earning $1.21 in year 2, it earned $2.21. In that case, the cumulative EPS would still be $5.10, and this method would still yield a 10 percent-per-year growth answer. You can see, therefore, that the cumulative method of measuring EPS growth is indifferent to the actual incidence of earnings; it is only the total that counts.

Looking back, most people would agree that if you are trying to incent truly long-term thinking, the cumulative method of measuring EPS growth would be preferred over all the other methods. It is straightforward; it doesn't come up with crazy answers like the percentage method; it takes account of all years in the performance measurement period; and it gives equal weight to each. It is because of these reasons that most companies that base performance share payouts on EPS growth use it.

On the other hand, the cumulative method does have one pitfall. Think about the fact that there are only two numbers involved. One is the $1 base-period number and the second is the $5.10 cumulative EPS number. Now it may take a lot of performance to change the second number, given that it is the total of four years of results. But the first number represents the EPS from only a single year. And from that perspective, a minor change in the first year's EPS figure can trigger a significant change in the answer. For example, assume that the company does indeed earn $5.10 over four years. But also assume that the base-period EPS figure is not $1 but $1.10. That scant difference of $0.10 per share in the base-period EPS figure has the startling effect of causing EPS growth to plummet from 10 percent per year to only 6 percent per year.

Although most companies use the cumulative method of determining EPS growth, other companies use other methods, including all the other methods described earlier. It is not important that you know precisely how to figure EPS growth, but know that there are different methods that can be used. That way, you can study your own company's method and, after factoring in your expectations as to future performance, you can assess the payout potential of the performance share grants you have received or those you are about to receive.

Is the base-period EPS figure always the EPS earned in the year preceding the beginning of a performance-measurement period?

No. The most common approach is to use a single-year base-period EPS figure. But because results can be skewed by a change in that base figure, as we have just learned, some companies employ a multi-year base-period approach. Hence, they do not measure EPS growth from the single year immediately preceding the start of a performance measurement period. Rather, it is measured from the simple average of the EPS earned in the two years immediately preceding the beginning of the period, or perhaps even from the three years preceding the start of the period.

This alternative approach is often preferred by companies with cyclical earnings patterns because it helps to even out swings in the base-period figure. It also has the advantage, usually unintended, of making the performance-share plan softer than it looks. Think back, if you will, about the EPS performance table showing a $1 base period EPS figure and a $5.10 cumulative figure. The figures in that table yielded a 10 percent per year EPS growth rate, figured on a cumulative basis (or any basis, for that matter). Now assume that, just as the company increased its EPS by 10 percent per year in future years, it also had been increasing its EPS at the same 10 percent-per-year rate in past years. On that basis, the EPS earned in the year immediately preceding the base year would have been $1/1.1, or $0.91. Hence, the average of the preceding two years' EPS would be $0.955. Now if the company actually ends up earning $5.10 cumulative EPS during the performance period, the EPS growth, figured any way except for the way the company figures it under its performance-share plan, will be 10 percent. But because the base-period EPS figure is only $0.955, not $1.00, the company will declare that it actually increased its EPS, not by 10 percent, but rather by a higher 12 percent per year. Indeed, if we could use a three-year average base-period figure, and assume that past EPS also increased at a 10 percent per year rate, we could turn what is really a 10 percent per year future EPS growth rate into a 13.9 percent future growth rate.

The use of these differing base periods underscores the necessity for you, as a performance share recipient, to understand exactly how your company's plan works. It may well turn out that the chances for a significant payout are much higher than would at first glance appear to be the case.

Do companies predicate long-term incentive payouts on measures other than growth in earnings per share?

Quite so. A minority of companies, but some, base payouts on average return on equity achieved during the performance-measurement period. For example, the company may specify that to earn all the contingently granted shares the return on equity must average 14 percent in after-tax terms during the four-year performance-measurement period. In effect, the company calculates its return on equity in each of the four years and then averages the four resulting return figures.

Some other companies prefer to base their payouts on return on capital employed. Here, the numerator of the fraction making up the return figure is the after-tax net income of the company plus the after-tax costs of any long-term debt charged against net income. The denominator is the sum of shareholders' equity and long-term debt. Companies in this category believe that a return-on-equity measure might cause senior executives to take on too much debt and, therefore, too much leverage. By employing return on capital employed, they figure that the executive will be indifferent to the source of capital and will have to earn the same return on incremental capital, whether that capital is equity capital or debt capital. They are right. Unfortunately, however, the executive is also made indifferent to borrowing costs as well, since interest payments are excluded from net income. This is not exactly a real-world approach, given the current high costs of borrowing.

A few other companies prefer to go all the way and incent return on assets. Generally, however, return on assets is not a popular choice except in companies, or entire industries, where return on assets is given great credence as a performance measure. Banking is one.

I've heard that some companies predicate long-term incentive payouts on how well they do compared to a group of other companies. How does this approach work?

Under this approach, the company avoids having to set any long-term performance targets. Rather, it defines its performance level on a relative basis—relative to how a group of similarly situated companies have performed during the same time period.

To illustrate, take the case of a commercial bank. Given that the bank's profits are going to be heavily influenced by interest rates, and given further that it is notoriously difficult to forecast with any precision the direction of interest rates over a long period of time, the bank decided to assess its performance, for long-term incentive purposes, on the basis of how well its return on assets over a five-year period compares to the return on assets of fifteen other major banks. If the bank achieved a return on assets that ranked at the median of the fifteen comparator banks, then executives earned 50 percent of the performance shares they had been contingently granted five years earlier. On the other hand, a 25th percentile or lower positioning vis-à-vis the comparator group brought a total forfeiture of performance shares, while a 75th percentile positioning resulted in a total earn-out of all the contingently granted shares.

What's wrong with using peer groups to measure company performance?

In some ways, nothing. But the company has to be sure that its comparator group is right for it. And it may find itself at the mercy of changes in accounting treatment by one or more of the comparator group companies—changes that are perhaps too subtle to detect from reading the annual report but that nonetheless have a significant impact on reported earnings in future years. It may turn out that one or more of the companies in the comparator group are merged into other companies, thereby disappearing from the group. Or, just the reverse— a company in the comparator group may buy some other company and so change the nature of the combined enterprise that it can no longer be considered an appropriate comparator group member.

Finally, we have the *reductio ad absurdum* argument. Suppose that every bank in your comparator panel earns a negative 1 percent on assets, but that your company earns a comparatively brilliant −0.5 percent return on assets. Because your company's performance places it on the 100th percentile of the comparator group distribution, a full payout of all contingently granted performance shares is made. To be sure, your bank outpaced the competition, but if you were a shareholder, would you feel like celebrating and offering your company's management a lot of extra money for its brilliant contributions?

Because of this logic flaw, some, but regrettably not all, companies with relative performance targets provide that no performance shares can be earned unless the company achieves some minimum absolute level of performance. Thus, if our hypothetical bank had stipulated that it would not pay out any performance shares, no matter what its competitive standing, unless it earned at least a 0.5 percent positive return on assets, then the potential problem would have been substantially mitigated.

On the other hand, suppose just the opposite happens. Your company's performance, while brilliant by the standards of every other industrial grouping, is lackluster compared to the companies in your particular comparator group. On that basis, you receive no performance shares at all, even though the shareholders, if asked their opinion, might have been quite content with the performance that had been delivered.

What about using more than a single performance measure in a performance share plan?

Some companies do use more than one measure. For example, a large industrial company predicates payouts under its performance share plan on both earnings-per-share growth and return on equity achieved during the performance-measurement period. In effect, the payout schedule is a matrix. By finding the intersection of your company's EPS growth and its return on equity, you determine the percentage of performance shares you stand to earn.

An approach like this can have real advantages. If your company has a high return on equity, you can receive a fairly substantial performance share payout even though EPS growth is fairly lackluster. On the other hand, if your company has excellent EPS growth but a poor return on equity, a substantial payout can also be earned. In effect, it takes both a low EPS growth rate and a low return on equity to trigger a zero payout.

Such a plan can also be in the shareholders' interests. After all, if the company lets its EPS drop from, say, $1 per share to $0.01 per share and then increases EPS to $0.02 per share, it ends up increasing EPS by 100 percent compared to the $0.01 per share earned in the base period. But from a real-world perspective, the company's performance is still deplorable in terms of return on equity. And since return on equity is one of the two measures governing payouts under the plan, executives in this company won't get away scot free.

What happens if my employment is terminated?

It all depends on the reasons for your termination. Generally speaking if you resign your employment voluntarily or are discharged for cause, you forfeit all your contingently granted performance shares. Discharge for cause, under the terms of most plans, is confined to things like putting your hand in the till.

On the other hand, if you retire in accordance with your company's retirement plan, are disabled, or die, you (or in the case of death, your estate) are often entitled to a pro-rata distribution of performance shares. Under a typical procedure, no payout is made until the end of the normal performance-measurement period. Then a determination is made as to how many performance shares you would have earned had you been employed throughout the performance-measurement period. Finally, that number of shares is multiplied by a fraction, the numerator of which is the number of months you served as an active employee during the performance-measurement period and the denominator of which is the number of months in the performance-measurement period itself. To illustrate, assume the performance-measurement period is four years and that you retire after two years. Assume also that two years after you retire, the company determines that 80 percent of all contingently granted performance shares have been earned, based on actual company performance during the four-year performance-measurement period. Assuming you had been contingently granted 1000 shares at the beginning of the performance-measurement period, you would, had you remained with the company for the entire four-year period, been entitled to receive 80 percent of those shares, or 800 shares. However, you served as an active employee only twenty-four months of the forty-eight month performance-measurement period. Hence, instead of receiving 800 shares, you receive half that number (24/48), or 400 shares.

Note that just because your employment is terminated doesn't mean that you need go away totally empty-handed. Note also that by using this approach, companies implicitly recognize that decisions being made today will likely have an impact several years from now. Accordingly, if you come to perceive that the results in the several years after you leave can cause your future compensation to go up or down, you will, hopefully, avoid the temptation to short-term it—for example, by maximizing the profits in your last year or two through huge cuts in the R&D budget. And you will be more motivated not to install some dummy as your successor—a person who will, through his or her failure, make you look good and enhance your niche in the corporate history book. Rather, you will look to the long-term needs of the business and take those actions that enhance your company's long-term viability.

There is one further type of termination of employment, and that goes under the euphemism *management-initiated termination.* In other words, you may have had your hands exactly where they should have been, but they weren't accomplishing anything, and so you got fired. This type of termination also goes by the name *discharge for other than cause* and by the even more unfortunate term *discharge without cause.*

One school of thought would invoke a full forfeiture of contingently granted performance shares. However, it is not infrequently the case that, although a person is being fired, the company feels a certain amount of compassion, for example, because the employee has long service. To turn around and kick the individual a second time by making him or her forfeit contingently granted performance shares seems, according to this view, to be unnecessarily cruel. Accordingly, the fired employee may well end up receiving some sort of pro-rata distribution, in much the same manner as if he or she had retired. Typically, such decisions are left to the board committee administering the plan.

What is restricted stock?

Restricted stock involves the grant of shares carrying restrictions against resale. Under a performance share plan, the company says to you: Deliver 12 percent per year EPS growth to us, and we will deliver to you 1000 free shares. In contrast, under one type of restricted stock plan, the company says to you: Here's 1000 free shares right now. If you don't deliver to us 12 percent per year EPS growth, you will have to return the shares to the company. In that sense, therefore, some types of restricted stock plans are nothing more than mirror images of performance share plans.

There are some additional advantages to a restricted performance share plan, as opposed to an ordinary performance share plan. One involves the fact that the terms of the restricted stock grant typically give you the right to receive the dividends declared on an equal number of common shares during the period the restrictions are in force. With performance shares, of course, you don't receive any dividends during the performance-measurement period. In addition, you usually get to vote the shares during the restriction period.

How much do I have to pay for restricted shares?

Usually nothing. In some cases, however, you are required to pay some nominal amount for the shares, say, $1 per share or the shares' par value of $0.10 each.

What do you mean by "restrictions against resale"?

During the particular restriction period, you cannot sell the shares except back to the company. And you cannot sell the shares to the company except under certain conditions. If those conditions obtain, you must sell the shares to the company. If you must sell the shares to the company, the sales price will equal what you paid for the shares, which may be nothing. Hence, if a sale (or what is termed a *forfeiture*) of the restricted shares occurs during the restriction period, you gain nothing from having held them, except for the dividends received up to the date of sale.

The events triggering a forfeiture of the restricted shares are the same events that would deny you any economic benefits from a performance share grant. Thus, if you resign from the company voluntarily or are discharged for cause during the restriction period, you will end up forfeiting your restricted shares. Or, perhaps you didn't resign, but the company didn't achieve its full performance goals. In that case, you will again have to sell some or all of the shares back to the company and thereby forfeit part or all of your economic benefit.

How long is the restriction period?

It depends on the particular plan. Generally, restrictions lapse all at once, either three, four, or five years after initial grant. But other patterns are possible, too. For example, one company causes the restrictions on 25 percent of the shares to lapse one year after grant; then at the end of each succeeding year, the restrictions on another 25 percent of the shares lapse. In another company, however, restrictions on the first 25 percent of the shares don't lapse until a date five years from the initial grant. In that company, the last of the restrictions do not lapse until eight years after grant.

What happens when the restrictions lapse?

You are then free to do with the shares what you will. You may sell them on the open market, keep them, give them to your children, and so forth.

Do I have to pay a tax when I receive restricted shares?

Surprisingly, only if you want to! The IRS gives you a choice, although it is very much of a Hobson's choice. Within thirty days of receiving a restricted share grant, you may elect to take into that year's ordinary income a sum equal to the fair market value of the shares on the date of grant, less the amount, if any, you paid for them. To illustrate, assume that you have received 1000 restricted shares at a time when the fair market value was $50 each and that you paid nothing for them. On that basis, you may, if you wish, take $50,000 into your ordinary income in the year of grant and pay taxes on that amount. By so doing, you establish a cost basis of $50 per share for each such restricted share. Then, when the restrictions lapse, you will owe no further tax; indeed, you will owe no further tax until you finally sell the shares on the open market. Should the stock have appreciated in value by the date of sale, then such appreciation (above your $50 cost basis) will be a long-term capital gain (assuming you have held the shares for six months or more). Should the stock have depreciated in value by the date of sale, the depreciation will represent a long-term capital loss (again assuming you have held the shares for six months or more).

But there's a catch to this election to pay a tax upon initial receipt of the restricted shares. Should you end up forfeiting some or all of the shares, you can kiss the tax you paid goodbye. The IRS will keep a viselike grip on your money.

When you combine this danger with the fact that to pay taxes upon initial receipt means you have to raise money through borrowings or the sale of other assets (remember, you can't sell the restricted shares, since they are restricted), few executives take advantage of the IRS's seeming generosity.

So if I don't pay a tax on grant of the restricted shares, when do I pay a tax?

If you don't elect to be taxed within thirty days of initial receipt of the restricted shares, you will incur no tax liability until the restrictions lapse. In that year, you will then have to take into your ordinary income a sum determined by multiplying the number of shares on which the restrictions have lapsed and the fair market value per share on the date the restrictions lapsed. Thus, if your 1000 restricted shares, which carried a fair market value of $50 each at the time they were initially granted, appreciate in value to $90 by the time the restrictions lapse, you will end up paying taxes at ordinary rates on $90,000. But by so doing, you establish a cost basis in the shares of $90 each and set the stage for capital gains tax treatment on any further appreciation or depreciation between the date the restrictions lapse and the date the shares are finally sold.

What about the dividends I receive? Are they taxable?

You bet! They are taxable as ordinary income in the year they are received.

Do all restricted shares require that certain performance goals be achieved?

No. There are a number of restricted stock plans that permit you to earn out restricted shares simply by remaining with the company during the restriction period. For example, if you remain with the company for five years, you will receive the full economic benefit from all the shares you are granted, even though the company has performed abysmally during the period.

To distinguish between these two classes of restricted shares, we will call those carrying performance restrictions *performance-lapse restricted shares*; and we will call those carrying no performance restrictions *time-lapse restricted shares*.

Earlier, we showed graphically the payout possibilities from 1000 nonqualified option shares and from 474 performance shares. Now let us add a line to that earlier graph (see Exhibits 10A, 10B, and 10C) and show what happens if we grant some time-lapse restricted shares. We will continue with the same assumptions used earlier, namely, that the initial fair market value at grant is $50 per share; that the company earns $5 per share in the year preceding the grant; that future EPS growth is 10 percent per year; and that the price/earnings multiple remains at 10x in all future years. We will also make some additional assumptions: The dividends per share in the year preceding grant were $2, or 40 percent of the EPS in that year, and the dividends per share in future years will equal 40 percent of the future EPS under the scenario being examined. On the basis of the above, we obtain the following results:

- Five years after grant, the fair market value per share will have appreciated from $50 to $80.53.

EXHIBIT 10A   Options, Performance Shares, and Restricted Shares

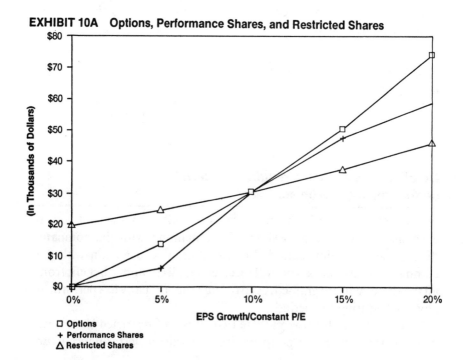

EXHIBIT 10B   Options, Performance Shares, and Restricted Shares

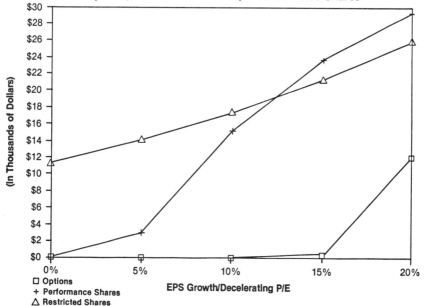

EXHIBIT 10C   Options, Performance Shares, and Restricted Shares

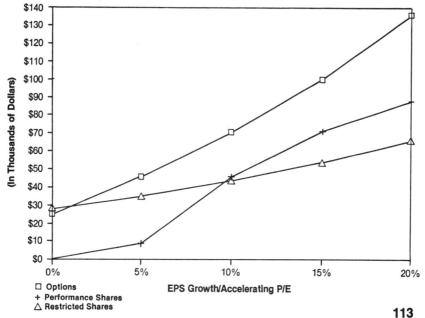

- Dividends per share will be $2.20 during the first year of the five-year restriction period, $2.42 during the second year, $2.66 during the third year, $2.93 during the fourth year, and $3.22 during the last year. Hence, total dividends per share will be $13.43.

- As a result, the total value per share, counting both the fair market value and the dividends received, will be $93.96.

- Recall that the value of the 1000 option shares at the end of the fifth year was approximately $30,500, and the value of the 474 performance shares contingently granted (of which only 80 percent were earned under this 10 percent EPS growth scenario) was also approximately $30,500.

- Accordingly, if we want to give an executive a total value of approximately $30,500 under the particular scenario, and if each time-lapse restricted share has a total value of $93.96, then we will have to grant him or her 325 shares ($30,500/$93.96).

You can see from the graphs that all three plans—the option plan, the performance share plan, and the time-lapse restricted stock plan—deliver the same $30,500 of economic benefit when future EPS growth is 10 percent per year and when the price/earnings multiple remains constant. But you can also see that when the future performance assumptions change, the payout profile of the time-lapse restricted stock grant differs markedly from that of the performance share grant and the stock option grant. When performance is poor, the time-lapse restricted stock grant is the clear winner. And when performance is superb, it is the clear loser (but only in comparative terms).

Time-lapse restricted stock makes for a beautiful holding device, if that's all the company wants to accomplish. When you think about it, the ability of a compensation device to cause you to remain with the company is in large part dependent on the probabilities you assign to receiving a payout and the sheer size of the payout being offered. On that basis, time-lapse restricted stock laps the field, because the probability of a payout is as close to 100 percent as you can get.

On the downside, however, you can also see that having once received a grant of time-lapse restricted stock, there may not be all that much of an incentive to work hard for the company. To be sure, an increase in EPS can bring about an increase in dividends per share (from which you benefit). And an increase in EPS can, if the price/earnings multiple of the stock behaves itself, lead to an increase in fair market value. But the number of shares granted to you will be relatively small, and because this is so, so will the extra payout for accomplishing extra results.

Do companies ever combine more than one type of long-term incentive device?

Yes. For example, one large bank offers its executives both stock options and time-lapse restricted shares. Typically, an executive receives three times as many option shares as he or she receives in time-lapse restricted shares. This particular blending gives the executive some downside protection through the restricted shares (and hence more holding power for the company) and more upside reward potential through the option shares (and hence more motivational impact for the company). Of course, the downside protection is not as great as that which could be obtained by granting 100 percent restricted shares; but the shareholder screams of giveaway will not be as great, either. And equally true, the upside reward potential is not as great as that which could be obtained by granting 100 percent stock options. But the executive is also given more protection in the event the price/earnings multiple—the one thing over which he or she has absolutely no control—should fall. So this type of combination plan represents a compromise, but a compromise in the best sense of the word.

Is time-lapse restricted stock taxed the same way as performance-lapse restricted stock?

Yes. There is no difference whatsoever.

A lot of companies grant something called "performance units." What are they?

Instead of offering you x shares for achieving certain performance goals, a company granting performance units simply offers you x dollars. In our earlier example involving performance shares, we assumed an executive had been contingently granted 474 shares at an initial fair market value of $50. Given 10 percent EPS growth performance, we went on to assume that he or she actually earned 80 percent of the shares, or 379 shares. These 379 shares had a final fair market value of $30,535.

Now, in Exhibit 11, let us again examine the payout curve of the performance shares. But this time, let us overlay on this curve the payout curve of a performance unit grant. Here, we will assume the

EXHIBIT 11A   Performance Shares Versus Performance Units

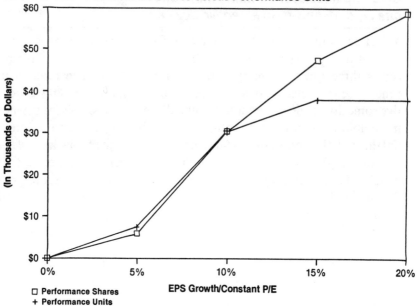

☐ Performance Shares
+ Performance Units

EXHIBIT 11B   Performance Shares Versus Performance Units

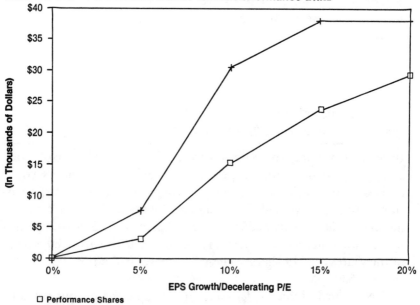

☐ Performance Shares
+ Performance Units

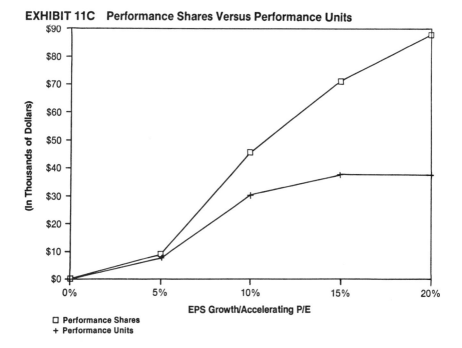

company offers an executive the opportunity to earn $38,169 in cash, provided EPS growth during a five-year period is 12 percent per year or more. For lesser amounts of EPS growth, the executive is promised various percentages of the $38,169 maximum award, as follows:

- Eighty percent if EPS growth during a five-year period is 10 percent per year.
- Twenty percent if EPS growth during the period is 5 percent per year.
- Nothing if EPS growth during the period is less than 5 percent per year.

Note that these are the same percentages of the maximum total award as were used earlier with performance shares. Only this time we are using dollars instead of shares. (Incidentally, the exotic $38,169 figure was derived working backwards, so that 80 percent of the figure would produce the same $30,535 payout as would be received from the performance share plan.)

You can see at a glance that performance units act differently from performance shares, even though the terms of earning them are substantially identical. This is because performance unit payouts are totally insensitive to what happens to the stock price in future years. If the stock price falls, the executive receives no less than if it had not fallen. And if the stock price rises, the executive receives no more than if it had not risen. As a result, the executive with performance units receives excellent protection in the event of a decline in his or her company's price/earnings multiple (but no extra reward in the event of an increase in the P/E multiple).

What are the tax consequences of performance units?

You pay no tax at all until you receive a payout. Then, in the year of the payout, you take the amount of the payout into your ordinary income.

Some performance unit plans involve payouts in company stock, instead of cash. What's going on here?

Not all that much. Going back to our earlier example, suppose that EPS growth turns out to be 10 percent per year and that the executive therefore qualifies for a payment of $30,535. And suppose further that the company wishes to make the payout in company shares. Accordingly, it will simply divide $30,535 by whatever is the share price at that time and deliver that number of shares to the executive. If, for example, the final share price is $75, the company will divide $30,535 by $75 and deliver 407 shares to the individual, plus an additional cash payment of $10 to cover the breakage.

Note the very significant difference between a performance share plan and a performance unit plan. Under a performance share plan, the executive receives 379 shares, the value of which is variable. But under a performance unit plan, the executive receives that number of shares that will have a value of $30,535. Hence, if the market price is not $75 at the end of the five-year performance period but rather is half that amount, or $37.50, the executive will receive 814 shares (plus $10 in cash), not 407.

So a performance unit plan that pays out in shares involves absolutely no market price risk for the executive—unless, of course, he or she decides to hold the shares after their delivery.

Granted that performance units insulate me from the stock market during the performance-measurement period. But if I receive a payout in shares and hold the shares, don't I take on a market risk?

Sure you do. But let's make a distinction here. I, the company, promised you $30,535 worth of shares if EPS increased 10 percent per year for five years. It did, and I gave you 407 shares because the then-fair market value was $75 per share.

Now let's assume that those shares are registered and that you can freely sell them. If you sell the shares the day you get them you're going to receive just about the $30,535 in cash I intended to give you. Now, if you decide not to sell the day you get the shares, is that my problem? Indeed, is that even my concern? By not selling immediately you made an investment decision.

Suppose, alternatively, that I had paid you $30,535 in cash and that you immediately bought 407 of our company's shares at $75 each. And suppose further that the shares promptly plummeted in value to $37.50 each. Would you be blaming me? I doubt it. So, if you decide to hold shares that you could have sold, that's no different from buying the shares for cash. On that basis, I won't take any credit for the fact that the shares appreciate from $75 to $100 if you won't give me any blame for the fact that the shares drop in value from $75 to $50!

If there is no market price incentive in a performance unit plan, why would a company want to make a distribution in shares?

For several reasons. First, the company may have a cash problem; by issuing shares, it conserves cash. Second, the company may want to raise some equity capital. By issuing shares, it achieves that goal. Third, the company may want to encourage you to become an owner, or a larger owner, of company shares. Sure, there may be no way for the company to force you to hold the shares (although a bit of informal jawboning is often quite effective, if you want to go places with the company). But by issuing shares, the company can capitalize on the principle of inertia. To raise cash, you have to stir yourself down to your broker's office, and that takes a certain amount of effort. So perhaps you will end up holding some or all of the shares.

Speaking of not selling shares, do some companies require you to hold on to shares acquired through option plans, performance share plans, and the like?

Yes, but happily not very many. Years ago, I remember hearing from an executive about a phone call he had received from his CEO. It seems the CEO had an interesting nocturnal habit: He liked to get into bed and pore over the stock transfer records of the company. In so doing, he discovered that the executive in question had just sold 5000 shares acquired a few weeks earlier through the exercise of a stock option. The CEO thereupon phoned the executive—at midnight—and said: "I just saw that you sold 5000 shares. Do that again, and you're finished!" The executive, who had been awakened from a sound sleep, thought he had been dreaming about the phone call from the CEO.

Continuing to own company shares is a noteworthy objective, but forcing people to do so can be fraught with problems. First, if an executive keeps borrowing and borrowing to hold on to shares, he or she must eventually run out of borrowing capacity. Yet if he or she has lots of unexercised stock options, how are those options ever going to be financed?

Second, we mentioned earlier that if you held on to company shares, you were making an investment decision and had to bear total responsibility as to future gains or losses. But we made this remark in the context of your being able freely to sell the shares upon their acquisition. Obviously, if you can't sell the shares, then all bets are off. Hence, if the shares should plummet in value after their acquisition, the loss thereby diminishes the value of your compensation package and makes it that much more likely that you will soon decamp for greener pastures—or at least for pastures where they don't require you to hold on to your shares.

Finally, forcing an executive to hold on to shares may, if things go well, leave him or her with an astonishing net worth. But if that net worth cannot be turned into a bigger house, the grand trip to Europe or a boat, then has it helped the executive, as opposed to his heirs?

Do some companies grant only performance units to their executives?

Yes, but very few. In theory, the idea of granting only performance units makes considerable sense, given that executives have no real influence over what happens to the price/earnings multiple. From that perspective, therefore, performance units represent a pure performance play, undiluted by the vagaries of the marketplace.

But suppose you are the CEO of a large company and you have just received a $1 million payout from a performance unit plan, due to the superb EPS growth your company has exhibited during the past five years. You find yourself at the annual meeting trying to answer an angry shareholder who has asked what you are doing about the deplorable price of the company's stock. What do you say? How about: Oh, is the stock price down? I'm sorry to hear that. You know, I don't own any shares anymore and my incentives have nothing to do with the price of the stock, so I rarely even bother to look up the price. In any event, I'm certainly sorry to hear the bad news, and I hope that the stock price will start to rise at the earliest possible opportunity. Give that answer and it may be your last annual meeting!

From a practical standpoint, therefore, it is the rare company that will go so far as to insulate totally its executives from the vagaries of the market price of its stock.

If a performance unit plan insulates the executive totally from the market price of the company's stock and if few companies permit total insulation, how does a market price incentive get injected into the proceedings?

Almost invariably, the garnish is a grant of some stock options. Earlier, we graphed out a 1000-share stock option grant, at an initial option price of $50 per share. Now let's start with this same payout curve in Exhibits 12A, 12B, and 12C. Then we'll overlay a second curve showing what happens with a combination grant of some option shares and some performance units. We'll work out the size of grant as follows:

EXHIBIT 12A   Option Shares Versus Option Shares and Performance Units

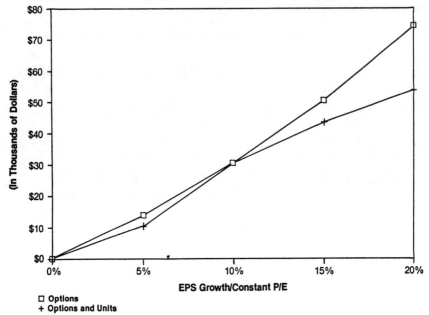

□ Options
+ Options and Units

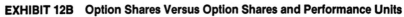

EXHIBIT 12B   Option Shares Versus Option Shares and Performance Units

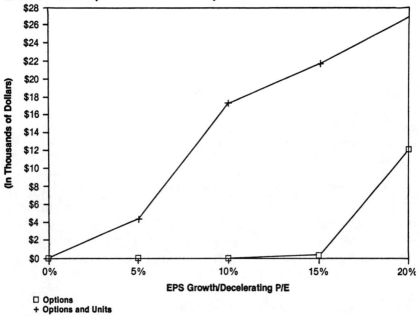

□ Options
+ Options and Units

122

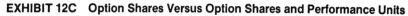

EXHIBIT 12C   Option Shares Versus Option Shares and Performance Units

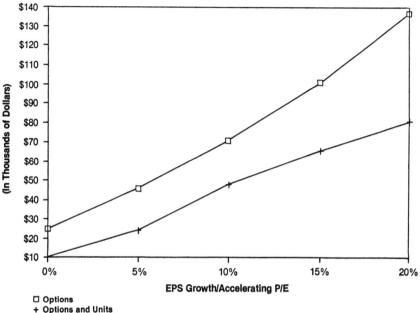

☐ Options
+ Options and Units

- Assume that we make the maximum unit value the same as the initial option price (which is a common approach). Hence, the maximum unit value will be $50 per unit granted, and the executive will earn that value when EPS growth during the five-year performance-measurement period is 12 percent per year or more.

- Unit payouts for less than 12 percent-per-year growth will be the same as described earlier for performance shares and performance units (80 percent payout for 10 percent growth, 20 percent payout for 5 percent growth, and no payout at all for less than 5 percent growth).

- Assuming 10 percent-per-year growth, the performance unit will therefore have a value of $50 × 80 percent, or $40.

- Again assuming 10 percent-per-year EPS growth and then going on to assume a constant price/earnings multiple, the fair market value of the stock will rise by 10 percent per year. Hence, the fair market value will rise from $50 to $80.53 at the end of the five-year performance-measurement period. Subtracting the option price of $50 yields a gain in the option of $30.53 per share.

- Hence, the total value of one performance unit and one option share, assuming 10 percent-per-year EPS growth and a constant price/earn-

123

ings multiple, will consist of the $40 value of the performance unit and the $30.53 value of the stock option share, or $70.53.

- If we want to give the executive a total payout of $30,525 at 10 percent-per-year EPS growth and a constant price/earnings multiple (the value of the 1000 option shares), we will need to grant the executive 433 stock option shares at an option price of $50 each, together with 433 performance units, with each carrying a maximum payout of $50. In that manner, the 433 option shares will yield a spread on exercise of $13,219 (433 × $30.53 per share), while the units will produce a payment of $17,320 ($50 per unit × 80 percent × 433 units). The total is $30,539.

You can see that the blending of stock option shares and performance units provides more protection against a declining price/earnings multiple than using stock options alone, but less protection than using performance units alone. On the other hand, it also provides less reward for an increasing price/earnings multiple than using stock options alone, but greater reward than using performance units alone. Hence, a blending of stock options and performance units represents sort of a middle-ground approach.

Is there really any difference between a grant of stock options and performance units and a grant of performance shares?

Under some scenarios, there is no difference. For example, if we assume 10 percent EPS growth and a constant price/earnings multiple, we know that both plans will pay out $30,535 in total economic benefits. But that is not the case with other scenarios.

In general, the combination of stock options and performance units is considered superior to the grant of only performance shares. This is for two reasons. First, under a performance share plan, you cannot receive any economic benefit until the end of the performance-measurement period. That is also true of the performance unit portion of a combination stock option/performance unit plan. But most companies permit you to exercise all, or at least a large portion, of the stock option shares prior to the end of the performance-measurement period for the units. Accordingly, the combination approach gives you more flexibility. If, for example, your stock price over time looks like the golden arches of McDonald's, you will, if you have great sagacity or plain luck, be able to exercise your stock option shares at a market high and yet still reap the benefit of the units at a time when, say, the market is down. Second, think about what happens with a performance share plan when actual performance is below the minimum performance required to earn any shares at all. You get nothing. That is also true of the performance unit portion of a combination stock option/performance unit plan. But with the latter, you still have your option shares. And even if they are worth nothing at the time, they typically carry a ten-year term, which means that you may have another five to seven years to reap some substantial gains should the fair market value of the stock turn up.

Finally, there is even an advantage to the company to using the combination approach. This involves the fact that charges to earnings under the combination approach can be lower than those required under a performance share plan. And even though the economic costs of the two plans may be identical, the fact that the accounting costs of one are lower than those of the other offers a company a powerful inducement to head for the combination approach.

With stock options and performance units, I have to pay for the options. But with performance shares, I get the shares free and pay nothing. Aren't I better off under the performance share approach?

True, you may have to pay for the stock options (although the company might give you a stock appreciation right in conjunction with the options, thereby eliminating the need for any payment at all). But you may have some help in the form of the cash you receive from the performance unit payout. Even if you don't have that source of cash, chances are you can borrow some cash for the short time required to exercise your options and then sell the stock.

So while the necessity to come up with cash with which to exercise your stock options may be a bit of a nuisance, it shouldn't represent any substantial burden.

I hear some companies give you stock options and performance units, but you can't have the benefits of both. What sort of deal is that?

Surprisingly, it might be a pretty good deal! Earlier, we discussed a company granting only stock options that offered a grant of 1000 shares at $50 per share. And we went on to talk about a company granting stock options and performance units that granted 433 stock option shares at $50 per share and 433 performance units with a maximum value of $50 each.

Now suppose a third company also granted an executive 433 stock option shares at an option price of $50 each and 433 performance units with a maximum value of $50 each. However, in this case, the company tells the executive the following: If you choose to exercise any of your stock options prior to the end of the five-year performance-measurement period governing your performance units, we will cancel one unit for each option share you exercise. Then at the end of the performance-measurement period, we will take one of two actions. If the value of the performance units exceeds the then economic benefit in your option shares (i.e., the aggregate fair market value of your option shares less the aggregate price you will have to pay to exercise them), we will pay out your units and cancel your option shares. On the other hand, if the economic benefit in your option shares equals or exceeds the value of your performance units, we will cancel your performance units, and you will continue to have the right to exercise your option shares during the remainder of their ten-year term.

There's no question that the deal just described is considerably inferior to a package involving 433 option shares and 433 performance units, where you get both components instead of only one of them.

However, suppose the third company sweetens the offer by granting 1000 option shares and 1000 performance units, with the executive receiving the economic benefits from only the options or the units. Exhibits 13A, 13B, and 13C show the payout curves for this approach and compare it to the payout curves for 1000 option shares alone and for 1000 performance units alone.

Note that when the price/earnings multiple drops, the either/or plan produces the same results as the performance unit plan. And when the price/earnings multiple stays the same or rises, the either/or plan produces the same results as the option plan. Hence, an either/or

EXHIBIT 13A Options, Units, and Tandem Options/Units

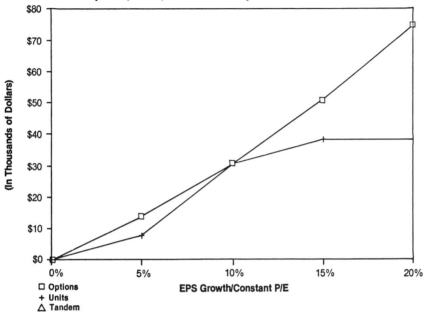

(In Thousands of Dollars)

EPS Growth/Constant P/E

☐ Options
+ Units
△ Tandem

EXHIBIT 13B Options, Units. and Tandem Options/Units

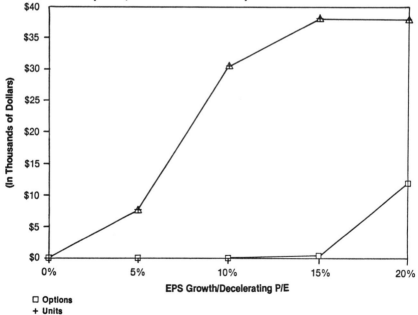

(In Thousands of Dollars)

EPS Growth/Decelerating P/E

☐ Options
+ Units
△ Tandem

127

EXHIBIT 13C   Options, Units, and Tandem Options/Units

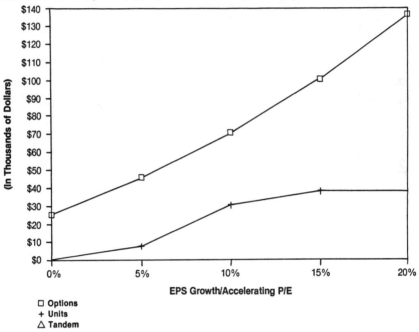

□ Options
+ Units
△ Tandem

approach represents the best of both worlds, provided you can receive enough shares and units.

Some companies, however, moderate the best-of-both-worlds aspects by making the maximum unit value less than the option price of the option shares. Hence, they may grant you 1000 option shares and 1000 performance units. But if the option price of the option shares is $50 per share, then the maximum price of the performance units may only be $35 per share. In this manner, the executive would pay an economic penalty if performance was good but if the market price of the stock dropped by, say, $15 between the time of grant and the end of the performance-measurement period.

Recently, a few companies have gone a step further with their either/or plans. Rather than making a decision at the end of the performance-measurement period to cancel the performance units or, alternatively, to cancel the stock option shares, they tell the executive the following:

At the end of the five-year performance-measurement period, we will determine the value of each of your performance units. We will

128

then open a deferred compensation account for you and credit you with this value. The sum credited will not earn interest and will not be paid to you until you request a payment. At that time, we will cancel the remaining option shares granted in connection with the performance units.

To illustrate, assume that company performance is such that you earn the maximum $50 per unit. As a result, we will credit your deferral account with $50,000. Then let us further assume that, during the five years remaining between the end of the performance-measurement period and the expiration of your stock option shares, the fair market value of our stock is such that your option shares are worthless. Accordingly, we will, upon the expiration of your option shares, give you a check for $50,000. Or, if you wish, you can call for the check earlier, but if you do, then we will cancel your option shares at that time. On the other hand, you may decide to exercise your option shares at some time during their remaining term. If you do, we will then cancel the $50,000 in your deferred compensation account.

Such an approach puts a floor under option gains. So if the executive is credited with $50 per performance unit, he or she is also being guaranteed that the economic benefits eventually to be derived from the option shares cannot amount to less than $50 per share. Of course, if the option shares appreciate to the point where the gain per share is, say, $100, the executive receives an even greater benefit (even though he or she ends up forfeiting the sum credited to the deferred compensation account).

I've heard talk about "book value stock." What's that?

First of all, let's define book value. Book value is simply another name for shareholders' equity (or net worth). Book value per share is the book value of the company divided by the number of shares outstanding. In theory, a business should be capable of being liquidated for its book value and the proceeds distributed to the shareholders.

A few public, as well as many private, companies permit an executive to purchase shares at the then book value per share. At some subsequent time, he or she then sells the shares back to the company for their then book value per share.

Granted an executive may benefit from an increase in book value per share. But how does the company achieve such an increase?

In most cases, by increasing its earnings per share and not paying out all the earnings per share in dividends per share. In effect, if a company earns, say, $5 per share and pays no dividends, its book value per share should increase by $5. And if it earns $5 per share and pays a dividend of $2 per share, its book value per share should increase by $3.

There are times, however, when the change in book value per share is not directly related to the company's EPS. For example, suppose a company has 10 million shares outstanding and a current book value per share of $50. On that basis, its total shareholders' equity is $500 million. Now assume that the current fair market value per share is a higher $100 and assume further that the company wishes to raise another $500 million in equity capital. On that basis, it sells a further 5 million shares to the public at $100 apiece to raise the needed $500 million. And when it is done, it has $1 billion of equity in the business and 15 million shares outstanding. And that being the case, its book value per share has risen from $50 to $66.67. (Now you begin to understand why companies hate to raise capital when their fair market value per share is lower than their book value per share. Under such a scenario, they would end up lowering their book value per share.)

However, even though not all changes in book value per share may be directly related to EPS, there is no question that EPS are the heavy-hitting determinant of book value per share.

If I have a grant of book value stock, it sure doesn't sound as if it's in my interest to see the company pay dividends. If it does, my book value rises more slowly, doesn't it?

Yes, it does rise more slowly. But remember that you, as a holder of the stock, receive the dividends. So from that perspective, you are better off with dividends being paid, because you get your returns earlier. On the other hand, the amounts paid in dividend are taxable as ordinary income, whereas had the company not paid the dividend, the increment could be taxed at long-term capital gains rates. Then, too, by retaining more profits in the business, the company might be able to increase its EPS at a faster rate in future years.

Can you say with certainty that using the book value per share as the measuring rod is a better deal for me than using the market value per share?

Indeed, it may not be a better deal. All that's happening here is that you are being insulated from changes in the price/earnings multiple of the publicly traded stock. Hence, a book value plan is very much like a performance unit plan.

However, a book value plan is also much softer than a performance unit plan. Under the latter, the company typically requires that some minimum EPS growth level be achieved before you receive anything. But under a book value plan, you are likely to receive some economic benefit as long as there are any earnings at all. For example, suppose a company earns $5 per share in the year preceding the grant of some performance units and then earns only $2 per share in each of the next five years. Under a performance unit plan, the payout is going to be zero, given that the company has probably mandated at least a 5 percent-per-year EPS growth rate to receive anything at all (much less receive the maximum unit value). But under a book value plan, the executive is likely to get $10 of economic benefit over the five years, since he or she typically receives an economic benefit equal to the company's entire earnings per share.

What are the tax consequences of book value shares?

The same as those involving any share purchase. Since you are required to sell the shares at their then-current book value per share (rather than their then-current fair market value per share), they cannot be worth more than their current book value per share at the time you purchase them. Accordingly, if the book value per share at the time of purchase is $50, and if you pay $50 for each share, you are paying full price. That being the case, you have established a cost basis of $50 per share in each share purchased. Then, when you sell the shares, you will have a capital gain or loss to the extent that the current book value is higher or lower than your purchase price. The gain or loss will be considered a long-term capital gain or loss, provided you have held the shares for at least six months.

Where am I supposed to get the money to purchase the book value shares?

Good question! If you have some other assets, you could sell them to come up with the funds required to purchase the book value shares. Or you could borrow the funds from a bank.

One aspect of the transaction you'll want to examine is the sort of yield you will be receiving on your investment. Since the purchase price is the book value, and since the book value might then be lower than the fair market value, you might find that your yield (i.e., the current dividends per share divided by your purchase price, with the answer multiplied by 100) is pretty good. Indeed, if the ratio of the book value per share to the fair market value per share is low enough, you might find that you are earning enough in dividends to pay the interest on your loan.

On the other hand, you might find just the opposite—the book value per share is higher than the fair market value per share. This raises an interesting question: If that is so, why do you want to purchase the shares in the first place? After all, you could get a higher yield by buying ordinary common shares on the open market. (Here, however, you might still conclude that the lower yield is offset by the fact that you don't have to worry about your investment being diminished because of swings in the uncontrollable price/earnings multiple.)

If I have to borrow funds to purchase my book value shares, why doesn't the company act as the lender?

You're getting into a tricky area here. First, let's talk about the reasons why your company might not want to lend you money; then we'll consider the other side of the issue.

Some companies are restrained by their state charters as to the amount of money they can lend to various employees. This is especially the case with banks, and it is sometimes the case with industrial companies when loans are being contemplated to senior officers. Second, even if the company can loan you the money, it must, if the shares are going to be used for collateral, follow pertinent Federal Reserve rulings regarding margin loans. This doesn't mean that the company must follow the margin rules exactly, but its ability to lend you anything it wants on whatever repayment terms it wants is impaired. Finally, even if there were no legal impediments to making a loan or Federal Reserve regulations to worry about, many companies are wary of granting loans because of what might be termed the *cosmetics*.

In the latter regard, we usually find that loans to executives are made at very favorable interest rates. That being the case, it is hard for the ordinary shareholder to understand how the company makes any money by borrowing funds from a commercial bank at, say, 12 percent interest and then promptly relending them to its top officers at, say, 9 percent interest.

Then, too, ordinary employees also have trouble understanding why the company should lend Mr. Big some money. After all, if anyone has the capacity to get his own funds, it is Mr. Big. And if anyone has some real need for funds, it is the ordinary employee.

The company and the executive must also be concerned with the fact that, under IRS regulations, a loan to purchase securities that does not carry at least a certain amount of interest will end up having interest imputed to it in the form of a discounted purchase price. The IRS reasoning basically goes like this: If I sell you some shares on an installment payment basis, and if I don't charge you a fair rate of interest, then, in present value terms, you are purchasing the shares for an amount lower than the amount you appear to be paying. In other words, part of your purchase price actually represents interest disguised as a purchase price. That being the case, you are actually buying the shares for less than they are worth, which means you may have to pay an immediate tax on part of the shares' then value.

OK, so maybe it's not such a good idea for the company to lend me money expressly for the purpose of purchasing shares. How about just having it lend me money, period? Then I'll use the money to buy the shares, but without pledging the shares as collateral.

If the company makes you an outright loan, that will solve at least some of the problems we have been discussing. Indeed, the company might even lend you the money at no interest.

Did you say a no-interest loan? That gets my attention!

It ought to! Yes, it is quite possible to make an interest-free loan to an executive.

You mean the IRS accepts a no-interest loan lying down?

Well, no. In fact, the IRS has been fighting no-interest and low-interest loans with a vengeance over the years.

The logic used by the IRS goes something like this: Suppose your company lends you $100,000 at no interest at a time when you would have had to pay 12 percent interest to any ordinary bank to secure the same loan. Now the IRS constantly espouses something called the doctrine of economic benefit. Simply stated, this doctrine holds that you must pay tax on all your income, even if some of it comes in nonmonetary form. Hence, just because I give you $10,000 of company stock as a bonus doesn't mean you can sidestep paying a tax on the $10,000; you did, after all, receive $10,000 of economic benefit—economic benefit that can, if you wish, be turned into cash.

On that basis, if your company lends you $100,000 at no interest when you would have had to pay a bank $12,000 in interest, did you not receive an economic benefit having a value of $12,000? You sure did. And no one disputes this contention.

Going one step further, the IRS contends that since you received an economic benefit of $12,000, you ought to increase your taxable income by the same $12,000 and pay taxes at ordinary rates on this sum. Given a 50 percent tax bracket, you would owe the government $6000 in taxes.

But if we are going to accept the IRS's argument that you would have had to pay the bank $12,000 in interest had you borrowed the $100,000 in an arm's-length transaction, wouldn't you then be able to deduct the $12,000 on your income tax return? And if that is so, wouldn't you end up owing nothing to the government, since you had an economic benefit of $12,000 and a tax deduction of a like $12,000?

Consider, for example, this alternative. Instead of lending you $100,000, the company tells you to go down to your friendly banker and borrow $100,000 at the usual 12 percent. To induce the bank to make the loan, the company even co-signs the note. Then, whenever you pay interest on the loan, the company gives you a cash bonus for the same amount. So you pay $12,000 in interest and the company promptly give you a $12,000 bonus. Here, clearly, you would have to take the $12,000 cash bonus into your ordinary income. But here, just as clearly, you would be entitled to a tax deduction for the $12,000 interest you paid. So you would have a wash.

Why the IRS refuses to see this logic escapes most rational observers. But the IRS, in a manner reminiscent of Don Quixote, picks up its lance every time it gets thrown and starts charging all over again. It has lost every lawsuit it has brought in this area (if not on original judgment, then on appeal). Indeed, it would still be tilting were it not for legislation passed by Congress in 1984. (We'll discuss this legislation momentarily.)

But even if we redesign the loan so as to sidestep Federal Reserve regulations and IRS requirements regarding unstated interest, what have we got? First, speaking for the company, someone's going to have to worry about whether you'll ever repay the loan. After all, you haven't pledged any collateral, and you could simply default and take the stock with you. Sure, we might get the shares back, or our money, after a lot of effort and a lot of time, but that's the problem—who wants to make the effort and take the time?

Second, what have we really done? We have, as just discussed, given you a sort of bonus equal to the spread between whatever the commercial lending rate is and the interest rate, if any, you are being required to pay. Perhaps if we simply offered you a real cash bonus in the same amount, you might well decide that you'd rather do something else with it than use it to buy the company's shares.

You mentioned some new legislation in the area of low- and no-interest loans. What effect will that have?

Under the new law, you will have to include in your ordinary income the value of any low- or no-interest loan. This value is determined by subtracting your actual interest rate from a rate stipulated by the government and then applying the difference to the outstanding principal sum of your loan. In turn, the rate stipulated by the government for 1984 is 10 percent; for 1985 and later years, it will most likely be the same rate the Federal government would have to pay to borrow funds with an equivalent maturity.

However, you will continue to be permitted to deduct any interest you have paid during the year, subject to certain limitations. And the amount you are now required to include in your income with respect to a low- or no-interest loan is considered to be interest paid.

Therefore, to the extent that your ability to deduct all interest expense you have incurred during the year is not impaired, this change in the law will have no appreciable effect.

For several years now, however, the law has provided that interest incurred for the purpose of making investments cannot be deducted if it exceeds the sum of $10,000 and the taxpayer's investment income for the year. In turn, investment income consists of items such as dividends, interest, rents, royalties, net realized short-term capital gains, and depreciation recapture gains. So, if you have borrowed a huge sum to buy company stock, and if the stock pays little or nothing in the way of dividends, you may find that a good part of any interest expense is not deductible in the particular year. Remember that an unrealized gain in the stock doesn't count for the purpose of determining how much interest you can deduct, nor does a realized long-term capital gain.

To the extent, therefore, that you report income because of the presence of a low- or no-interest loan, and to the extent that you cannot take an offsetting deduction, then to the same extent, you have had it! (The amount of nondeductible interest expense may yet become deductible in a future year, but losing the deduction now sort of takes the fun out of the game.)

At any point in time, the company has some extra funds lying around. That being the case, am I right in assuming it costs the company nothing to lend me some of those funds until it needs them?

That's faulty reasoning. No matter how you slice it, the company incurs a cost to make you the loan. If it doesn't have the funds lying around, as you put it, it will have to borrow them and pay interest itself. There's real cash going out. If it does have the funds lying around, they really aren't lying around. At the least, they are sitting in some sort of money market account earning interest. So if the funds are withdrawn and lent to you at no interest, there's real cash not coming in. And real cash not coming in is just the same as real cash going out.

*The company could accept my note for a
loan and then issue me some stock. Is
there something wrong with reasoning that
the exchange of pieces of paper
carries no real consequences?*

Nothing, except that the company, as you put it, has to issue some paper. That means that every time it computes its earnings per share, it must divide its earnings by all the shares it formerly had outstanding—plus the shares it just gave to you. So it may be true that there's no cash drain here. But there sure is some dilution.

*So when all is said and done, there's no
such thing as a free lunch, is there?*

One could do worse than accept that statement as a working hypothesis!

*Going back to book value shares, when do
I have to sell them back to the company?*

Perhaps only when your employment with the company is terminated. Or perhaps the company will require that shares be resold at fixed intervals, for example, five years after their initial purchase by you.

*Instead of going to the trouble of having
me purchase the book value shares and
then sell them back at some future time,
how about having the company just pay me
the difference in share prices? Wouldn't
that be a lot simpler?*

In some ways, yes. The company can certainly have a so-called phantom version of a book value stock plan. As you suggest, the company would grant you some units, with the initial price of each unit equal to the then book value per share. Then, on some future date, the company would pay you the amount, if any, by which the then book value per share exceeded your initial unit price, multiplied by the number of units granted. The payment would most likely be in cash, but it could be in a number of shares having the same cash-equivalent value.

One design problem under such a plan involves what to do about dividends. Do you receive phantom dividend payments (i.e., a cash payment equal to the dividends you would have received had you been an actual shareholder)? If you don't, it would appear that you will lose out, since any monies paid in dividends generate no economic benefit for you.

With a phantom book value plan, one approach is to pay phantom dividends. But a second approach is to wait until the units are redeemed and then add to any amount payable to the executive a further amount equal to the aggregate dividends declared on a like number of common shares during the period the units were in force.

What's the tax treatment of phantom book value shares?

The same as ordinary cash. In effect, whenever you receive a payment, you take that payment into your ordinary income.

The tax treatment for phantom book value shares doesn't sound as appealing as the tax treatment for outright book value share purchases. With the latter, you get long-term capital gains tax treatment, right?

Right! Let's review the two transactions. Under the first, the company sells you $100,000 of book value shares. You pay $100,000 at the time of sale and hold the shares for five years. Assume that no dividends have been declared and that the shares are worth $250,000 at the end of five years. You then sell the shares to the company and realize a $150,000 long-term capital gain. Given that you are at a 50 percent tax rate for ordinary income, your long-term capital gains tax rate will be 20 percent, and you will pay $30,000 in taxes. As a result, you will net $120,000 from the transaction on an after-tax basis.

Now let's rerun the transaction on a phantom basis. You receive a cash payment equal to the $150,000 aggregate spread in your phantom units. But this time you must pay taxes at ordinary rates and so you net only $75,000 after taxes.

So, from a tax standpoint, you are clearly better off with real book value shares than with phantom shares. But consider other factors. First, with real book value shares, you have to lay out some cash. If the dividends you receive don't cover your interest payments, you will sustain a negative cash flow. Second, think about what will happen if the book value per share should plummet instead of advance. That may well be an unlikely possibility, but in some companies, huge write-offs are taken from time to time. Even though the company becomes profitable again in short order, the damage to book value per share lasts a long time. In such an instance, the holder of real shares sustains a real loss. Thus, if you pay $100,000 for shares and end up having to sell them back to the company for $50,000, there's no way you're not going to be out of pocket $50,000 (on a pretax basis). But if you have $100,000 worth of book value units and their value drops to $50,000, you may not make anything, but you won't lose anything either.

Finally, although there may be a tax advantage to you from real book value shares, there is a corresponding tax disadvantage to the company. Take that $150,000 economic benefit we were just discussing. If the benefit arises from real book value shares, the company is denied any tax deduction, but if it arises from phantom book value shares, the entire $150,000 amount is deductible. So in the first case, the $150,000 benefit costs the company $150,000; in the second case, assuming the company is at a 46 percent marginal tax rate, the $150,000 benefit costs the company 54 percent of $150,000, or $81,000.

In recent months, a lot has been written about something called "junior stock." What's that?

Suppose your company's common stock is currently trading at $50 per share. Suppose also that your company wishes to create a separate class of common stock, with these attributes:

- You will have to purchase the shares right away.
- The dividend rate is only half that applicable to the regular common stock.
- After purchasing the shares, you cannot sell them to anyone.
- However, if you remain with the company for five years and if the EPS growth during the period is at least 10 percent per year, then at the end of the period the shares will be exchanged, for regular common shares, on a share-for-share basis.

Now, if you were looking at this second, or junior, class of stock critically, would you think it would be worth $50 per share, the same price as the regular common, which, after all, is freely saleable, carries the full dividend, and is not hemmed in by restrictions as to continued employment and restrictions as to future performance? If you answer yes to this question, perhaps you'll want to turn to some other book for amusement—like *Dick and Jane Go to Fantasyland*.

Well, that's just the point. The junior common stock cannot be worth the same amount as the regular common stock. So what you first need to do as a company is to get someone with expert credentials to validate your instinctive belief.

Enter the Wall Street investment banker. After spending years trying to assure clients that their stock is worth a great deal more than anyone seems to be willing to pay for it, he or she is perhaps not as nimble-footed as necessary when learning that what the client wants this time is to be told how worthless are these junior common shares. But don't count out Wall Street investment bankers when it comes to adapting to change.

In short order, therefore, the investment banker opines that the junior common shares are worth only, say, one-tenth as much as the regular common shares. Hence, given a regular common share market value of $50, the junior common shares are worth only $5 each. The first piece of the puzzle is now in place.

Next, the company turns to its tax lawyers. The trick here is to assure that, if the junior common shares are ultimately exchanged for regular common shares, the exchange will be considered a tax-free exchange. Hopefully, the company will receive such an opinion from its tax lawyers (who will, if necessary, try to obtain a private ruling from the IRS).

Finally, the company turns to its accountants. Since its investment bankers have stipulated that the shares are worth only $5 each and since the executive will pay $5 each to purchase the shares, the company will argue that any gain the executive eventually receives should not be considered a compensation cost; hence, there should be no charges to earnings required.

Now let's assume that all three ships come in for the company. Its investment banker sees the shares as being worth only $5, its tax attorney smells a tax-free exchange, and its accountant cannot possibly see how this transaction can have anything to do with compensation. That being the case, the company then offers to sell you 1000 junior common shares at $5, with all the restrictions just mentioned hung on the purchase.

Let's assume the company satisfies its investment bankers, its tax lawyers, and its accountants and goes on to sell me some junior stock. Where do I go from there?

That depends. Let's look at two forks in the road. Under the first fork, all the conditions precedent to the exchange into regular common are satisfied and an exchange takes place at the end of five years. And under the second fork, all the conditions are not satisfied and no exchange takes place.

Starting with the first fork, let's assume that the regular common stock, which had a fair market value of $50 per share at the time the junior common shares were sold to you, appreciates in value to $150 per share at the time the tax-free exchange takes place.

That being the case, you turn in your junior shares and receive 1000 regular common shares, with a current aggregate fair market value of $150,000. Given that you paid $5000 for the 1000 original junior common shares, you are now sitting on a gain of $145,000, which is not a bad return for a paltry $5000 investment.

You won't have to pay any tax on the $145,000 gain until you sell the regular common shares. But let's assume you do just that right after the conversion. Since you had held the junior common shares for more than six months prior to their conversion, you will receive long-term capital gains tax treatment on the entire $145,000 gain. So, assuming you are at a 50 percent tax rate for ordinary income, you will end up paying a 20 percent tax on the $145,000 gain, or $29,000. Hence, you will be left with $116,000 of tax-free money.

Now let's take the other fork—the one where some or all of the conditions precedent to the tax-free exchange are not satisfied. The conditions of the transaction might render your 1000 junior common shares worthless. And if that is the case, you have just lost $5000. That $5000 can be written off your taxes, however, although given the time you probably held the shares, the loss will be a long-term capital loss.

In some cases, the company might repurchase the junior common shares at the same $5 price you paid for them. In that case, you would come out even, although you might have sustained an opportunity cost if the dividends you received were low in comparison to what you might have gained by investing the $5000 in some alternative medium or in comparison to the interest you paid if you borrowed the money to purchase the junior common shares.

Wow! Junior stock's pretty good, isn't it— getting a $145,000 gain and paying only 20 percent tax to boot?

It certainly seems to be. But consider the fact that the company also doesn't receive any tax deduction, either.

Now let's structure a somewhat different incentive plan. The company tells you this: You are hereby granted 1600 phantom stock units. Each of them entitles you, five years from now, to a payment equal to the amount, if any, by which the fair market value of our common stock at that time exceeds $5 per share. In the event, however, that you don't remain with the company during the five-year period or in the further event that the company fails to increase its EPS by at least 10 percent per year, then all bets are off, and you won't receive anything from your 1600 units.

Now let's examine this transaction using the two forks in the road discussed earlier for junior common stock. First, we will reverse the order and look at the second fork—the one where some or all the precedent conditions are not satisfied. In this case, you end up receiving nothing. But that's better than losing $5000, don't you agree?

Second, we come to the first fork; all the precedent conditions have been satisfied. Given that the fair market value of the common stock has advanced from $50 to $150, and given further that you are entitled to a payment above $5 per share, you receive a $145 cash payment for each of your 1600 phantom units; hence, you receive a check for $232,000 for all 1600 units.

You then take this $232,000 into your ordinary income and pay a 50 percent tax on it. You are left with $116,000 in tax-free dollars. And that is the same place you ended up with junior common stock!

Note that you avoided having to shell out money at the time of grant. And you avoided having to read the eyestraining print surrounding the purchase and possible exchange of the junior common shares. And you avoided paying legal fees to defend yourself in case your friendly, and very local, IRS agent never heard of junior common stock and figures you're trying to euchre The Service.

For its part, the company had to lay out $232,000 instead of $116,000. But the $232,000 is fully deductible, and so, assuming a 46 percent tax rate for the company, the cost is only 54 percent of $232,000, or $125,280. When all is said and done, the net cost to the company for putting $116,000 of tax-free funds in your pocket has dropped from $145,000 to $125,280.

So if the whole idea of junior stock doesn't make a lot of sense, why is there so much enthusiasm for it?

Perhaps the great appeal is the belief that somehow there really is a free lunch. After all, if you look only at the executive's side of the transaction, ordinary income is, almost alchemistically, being transformed into long-term capital gains income. And as to the loss of the company's tax deduction, that's the company's problem! In effect, when the transaction involves someone else's cost and your benefit, maybe you don't spend all that much time doing rigorous cost analyses.

But what about those fledgling high-tech firms? Surely, junior common stock ought to make sense there?

That's what many people say. The argument goes like this: The baby high-tech firm has an almost inexhaustible ability to turn out share certificates (nowadays, it can use its own technology and employ laser printers), even though it is short on cash. And we've all heard how getting in on the ground floor with the stock can make a person a millionaire overnight. Besides, the company doesn't lose its tax deduction; it has no taxable income because sales are currently only $1 million and costs are currently $50 million.

Although all this may be true, the use of junior common stock may still not make much sense. If the company is short on cash, it can issue some nonqualified stock options. If the company has not yet gone public, the option price of the stock options can be set to equal the current book value per share or some other reasonable measure. And the timeframe of the stock options can be set long enough so that the company will have gone public before the options expire.

On that basis, the executive will not have to lay out any money to purchase the shares at the time of grant. If the company never goes public, the executive may still make some money by exercising the options (e.g., the book value may have increased in the meantime). If the company does go public, the options may take on tremendous value. They can be exercised and, if necessary, sold right away to produce a cash bonanza. To be sure, the executive will be taxed at ordinary income rates, but one assumes the company, which benefits by a tax deduction, will be willing to make it worthwhile for the executive by granting him or her approximately twice as many non-qualified stock option shares as it would have granted in junior common shares.

Finally, we have the issue of the company's tax deduction itself. To be sure, the company is now operating at a loss, and so any extra tax deductions would seem to be superfluous. But will the company still be operating at a loss, say, ten years from now when the options are about to expire? If it is, then one might wonder just how much the stock will be worth anyway. And although the company does sustain a tax loss in the year of option exercise, the loss can be carried forward for up to fifteen years. Accordingly, the use of junior stock would appear to be questionable even in a high-tech environment.

So if I'm offered some junior common stock, I should turn my back on it, right?

Well, we wouldn't go that far! If the company wants to give you a deal while shafting itself, that's not really your concern, is it?

If the company persists in using junior stock, could it give it to me in the form of an incentive stock option?

Yes, that could probably be arranged. There would be two advantages compared to an outright purchase of junior stock. First, you wouldn't have to lay out any money at the time of grant. Because this is so, you would never be in the position of sustaining an outright loss of, say, $5000 (assuming the alternative would be to purchase 1000 junior common shares at $5 each). Second, because the price is so cheap ($5 per share), you can receive an option on as many as 20,000 shares in a single year. (Remember, the maximum regular grant under an ISO plan can't exceed $100,000 of shares per year.) That compares to only 2000 shares, assuming that another alternative would be to grant you a regular ISO, with the regular common stock then selling at $50 per share.

But, no matter how you slice it, we're right back in the soup again when we confront the fact that the company loses its tax deduction. The transaction is simply not cost-effective, compared, say, to granting a larger number of nonqualified stock option shares.

Nevertheless, if the company absolutely insists in turning its back on a handsome tax deduction, the grant of an ISO in junior common shares could have substantial appeal compared to having to purchase the shares outright at the time of grant.

Given all the problems discussed above, what do you see as the future of junior stock?

Frankly, I see junior stock as being a fad, which will shortly disappear from the compensation landscape. As of this writing, the accounting fraternity is already beginning to exhibit second thoughts about its willingness to let a company sidestep all charges to earnings for the junior shares. Should the accountants reverse themselves and demand full charges to earnings, the lust for junior stock will abate very quickly.

One also has to wonder about the IRS. Of late, The Service has begun to refuse to offer advance rulings on various stock plan transactions. Should that prove to be the case with junior stock plans, then the executive, as well as the company, will be forced to sail in the dark. Perhaps a tax-free exchange, years after the initial purchase of junior shares is made, will go unchallenged by the IRS. But then again, perhaps it won't.

Long-term incentive plans that pay out on the basis of, say, long-term growth in corporate EPS may be fine for someone with corporate-wide responsibilities. But suppose I work in a division or subsidiary of a company? What happens then?

In most cases, your long-term incentive payouts are based on the results of the corporation, not on the results of your division or subsidiary.

That's a pity if you're running a clean profit center that is one of many profit centers within your company, because much greater motivation could be obtained by offering you a long-term incentive payout based on the long-term results of your division or subsidiary.

What do you mean by a "clean profit center"?

A clean profit center is one that could be divested to your company's shareholders tomorrow and would survive quite handily. If the division is involved in, say, the hardgoods industry, it has a manufacturing function; it has a sales and marketing function; it has a research function; it has a finance function; and so on.

Besides having all its vital organs, a clean profit center should also do little business with the other profit centers of the company. If that is not the case, then we probably have some *transfer pricing problems*, that is, problems centering around the establishment of a fair price that the selling division charges the buying division.

If a profit center doesn't meet all the criteria just enumerated, it would be difficult to establish viable long-term incentive programs for it.

Well, there are lots of clean profit centers in lots of companies. So how come few companies have chosen to set up long-term incentive plans that pay out on the basis of profit center results?

Several reasons. The first is sheer laziness. It takes a lot more work to set up, say, ten different long-term incentive plans in a corporation than only one.

Second, there is often the fear that, with divisional long-term incentive plans, some profit center executive might do so well that he or she would end up receiving more long-term incentive compensation— or, worse, more total compensation—than the CEO would. That's a real no-no in most corporations. CEOs may have no choice about being insecure over some things, but the CEO likes to go to bed at night secure in the knowledge that he or she is indeed the highest-paid employee in the company.

Third, we have some real problems in establishing valid long-term incentive targets for a division or a subsidiary.

Why are there so many problems in establishing valid long-term performance targets for divisions and subsidiaries of a company?

First, divisions and subsidiaries don't have a market price that can be used for long-term incentive measurement purposes. What is more, it is difficult to get any sort of valid EPS-like measurement. However, proxies can be devised for both measures, if one wants to take the time.

Second, suppose you could get an EPS-look-a-like measure for a division or subsidiary. Would you then establish the same EPS growth targets for every division/subsidiary in your company as for the company itself? If you did, you would probably find that the distribution of long-term incentive payouts among different divisions/subsidiaries would be awesome. For example, what about the new baby division that is entering a whole new field? For the next few years, it may be programmed to lose money. If so, its EPS growth can't even be measured. On the other hand, another division may have passed its developmental phase and is now coining money. For that division, the payouts would be gargantuan.

Handling matters this way may not necessarily be wrong, but you had better be prepared for the destruction of what you heretofore thought of as corporate internal pay equity.

As an alternative, you could try to shape the various EPS growth targets to match the phase of its life cycle in which the division finds itself. So, even though a maximum payout will be made for 15 percent corporate EPS growth, an EPS growth of, say, 30 percent may be required for a maximum payout in the case of Division A, while an EPS growth of only, say, 5 percent may be required for a maximum payout in the case of Division B. On its surface, the assignment of such disparate targets may seem unfair, but it may be the case that each division will have to stretch just as much as the other to reach its assigned targets.

So, there are apt to be some problems in establishing divisional performance targets for long-term incentive plans. But, with a good-faith effort, the job is not impossible to accomplish.

Do you favor greater use of divisional long-term incentive plans?

Yes. Some companies are so huge that to offer an executive a long-term incentive based on the overall corporation's results is not much different from offering him or her different levels of pay depending on how much real GNP growth is exhibited by the U.S. economy. In both cases, there is little, if anything, the executive can do to affect the outcome. Therefore, the long-term incentive plan is not motivational in any meaningful sense of the word. Worse, since short-term incentive payouts may well be influenced by divisional performance, the executive may end up deciding that the best way to maximize his or her income is to exhibit decidedly short-term behavior and hype up the division's current results. After all, if the division falls apart three years from now, that's no real problem if you've already been promoted based on what looked at the time to be marvelous performance. Indeed, the fact that your former division falls apart after you've left enhances your legend even further. And, if your colleagues running the other divisions have not been so imprudent as you and have looked to the long-term viability of their businesses, you can get even greater rewards through the corporate long-term incentive plan.

It seems to us, therefore, that a better way to proceed in the case of a truly clean profit center is to design a viable long-term incentive plan based on that profit center's long-term results. Payouts should be geared to performance that is demonstrably in the shareholders' interests. And, equally as important, the incentive opportunity ought to be unlimited. If the plan is designed right and if the divisional executive makes more than his or her CEO, then all that has happened is that he or she has way outperformed the CEO.

Although few companies now have divisionalized long-term incentive plans, what's the direction of the trend?

A small but growing number of companies are beginning to take action on this front and to introduce divisionalized incentive arrangements for at least some of their divisions.

For example, one company recently offered a group of executives running a particular division a pot of money determined as follows:

1. From the division's net income each year for the next four years, deduct a sum determined by multiplying the division's beginning-of-the-year capital investment by 12 percent. Thus, if net income for year 1 is $50 million and capital investment as of the beginning of the year is $300 million, then $36 million ($300 million × 12 percent) will be deducted from the $50 million in profits, yielding a $14 million surplus.

2. Add together the four figures from step 1. If the result is a number less than zero, change the number to zero.

3. Take 10 percent of the figure in step 2. This is the incentive fund for the entire group of executives.

The plan goes on to provide that various executives receive various percentages of the pot.

Here we have a simple, but a potent, long-term incentive plan. No rewards will be paid unless the division earns a minimally acceptable return on capital over a period of years. Once that minimal return has been generated, then $0.10 out of every extra dollar goes into the incentive fund. And there is no limit to the size of the incentive fund.

You can bet that the executives in this division are working very hard to produce magnificent long-term results; if they do, they stand to earn magnificent compensation.

SECTION FOUR

EXECUTIVE BENEFITS

A decade ago, yet another type of executive compensation emerged—benefits that are extended only to executives, not to employees generally.

These come in many types and can be quite valuable. Consider these points:

- Unless your company takes some positive action, you could find that the pension you thought you were going to receive has been drastically reduced, courtesy of your friendly Congress.

- Many companies now predicate pensions not only on the base salary you earned during the last few years preceding your retirement, but also on any short-term bonuses you earned during the same years.

- Some companies are willing to give you a "pension deal" when you join the company. In effect, they end up treating you, for pension purposes, as if you had been with the company for some time prior to the time you actually joined.

- As an executive, you may be entitled to extra amounts of life insurance coverage. Moreover, most or all of your life insurance coverage will not be reduced after you retire. That being the case, you are guaranteed an instant estate.

- A number of companies are willing to see that you incur not one cent of medical expense for yourself or your dependents. And by "medical expense," the company also means dental expense, psychiatric expense, vision care expense, and virtually any other expenses that can remotely be considered to have something medical going for them.

- An increasing number of companies are willing to offer you protection—sometimes wildly generous protection—in the event that a predatory company gobbles up your company. You may well find that the new owners don't even need to move on you before you can move on them and cart away a truckful of money.

I understand that the government has taken some sort of action to limit the amount of pension a person can receive. Is that really true?

Yes, it is. The first limitation occurred under the Employment Retirement Income Security Act—better known as ERISA. Under that law, the pension under a *defined benefit plan* (one where, for example, the executive receives a pension equal to 2 percent of his or her final five-year average salary, multiplied by the number of years of service) was limited to $75,000 per year.

However, the $75,000 cap was permitted to increase each year according to changes in the Consumer Price Index, with the result that it reached approximately $135,000 by 1982.

Then the government passed a new law, one part of which reduced the ERISA cap to $90,000 per year and provided no further cost of living escalation until 1986.

Suppose that my company's pension plan is designed to offer me 50 percent of my final salary when I retire and that my final salary will be $300,000. In that case, I'm supposed to receive a pension of $150,000. Now are you telling me that I can't get more than $90,000?

You're a quick study! The fact is that you will be limited to a pension of $90,000 from your company's qualified pension plan unless your company does something about it.

What can the company do?

Well, it could adopt what has come to be known as an ERISA Excess Plan. Under such a plan, the company would tell you the following: Because of governmental limitations, we can pay you a pension of only $90,000 from our qualified pension plan. However, we will also pay you an additional amount of $60,000 per year from our ERISA Excess Plan. So when you add up both payments, you will still receive a pension of $150,000 per year.

Will the ERISA excess pension payment be taxed any differently from the regular pension payment?

No. Both payments will be taxed at ordinary income rates.

So, leaving aside the fact that I get two checks, what's the difference between a regular pension plan and an ERISA Excess Plan?

There are two differences, one of which has little impact on you as an individual; the second may have a decided impact, though the probabilities are likely to be low.

Under a qualified pension plan, a company gets an immediate tax deduction on any monies paid to the qualified pension trust. Hence, if the company contributes $50,000 to the trust on your behalf, it gets to deduct the $50,000 right away, even though you won't receive any benefits for many years. In contrast, almost all other compensation payments, including the payments made under an ERISA Excess Plan, are deductible to the company only in the year the actual payment is made to you. So from a cost-effectiveness standpoint, payments made under a qualified pension plan are preferable to those made under an ERISA Excess Plan.

Second, payments made to a qualified pension trust actually leave the company's balance sheet and go to a bank, an insurance company, or some other fiduciary. Because this is so, your company could go belly up and yet your pension would still be protected. In contrast, an ERISA Excess Plan requires that funds be held in the company as part of the company's unsegregated assets. Therefore, a bankruptcy on the part of the company could jeopardize your ability to receive payments under the ERISA Excess Plan. In effect, you would become a general creditor of the company and would have to stand in line behind a number of other creditors, including the banks.

Do a lot of companies have ERISA Excess Plans?

Virtually all large companies have them, and many smaller companies as well.

**My company provides a pension benefit of
50 percent of final base salary if I am
employed for twenty-five years before
retiring. Why can't the benefit be 50 percent
of my final total compensation, including
my bonus, instead of being predicated only
on base salary?**

It can be. Some companies do apply the retirement percentage (say, 50 percent) to the sum of your final average base salary and your final average annual bonus. They do this as part of the regular qualified pension plan.

However, there aren't many companies in that category, because defining pensionable pay as being total compensation can often cause pensions to be based not only on executive bonus payments, but also on lower-level employees' overtime payments, supper money allowances, and so forth. This is because the IRS insists that no qualified pension plan be permitted to discriminate in favor of higher-salaried employees. But there are quite a few companies that handle this problem through what is called a Supplemental Executive Retirement Plan (SERP).

What's a supplemental executive retirement plan?

Under a SERP, the company will first probably incorporate the ERISA Excess Plan discussed earlier. Then the company will go further—for example, by defining pensionable earnings to include final average bonus payments. To illustrate what happens, let us see what a company says to its executives under its SERP: If you have twenty-five years of service upon your retirement, we will give you a pension equal to 50 percent of your final average salary plus 50 percent of your final average bonus. Assume that your final average salary is $300,000 and that your final average bonus is $150,000. Hence, assuming you have twenty-five years of service, your total pension will be 50 percent of $450,000, or $225,000.

Our qualified pension plan provides a benefit of 50 percent of final average salary for twenty-five years of service. So, ordinarily, your pension under this plan would be equal to 50 percent of your final average of $300,000, or $150,000. However, since this pension level exceeds the $90,000 amount we can pay by statute, you will be receiving only $90,000 from our qualified plan. The remainder of your $225,000 total pension, or $135,000, will be coming from our SERP.

A SERP typically talks in terms of a total benefit, part of which will be paid out of a qualified pension plan and part of which will be paid from the SERP itself.

That sounds pretty good. But if the company is going to make my bonus pensionable, what happens if performance is so poor during my final years with the company that I receive no bonus?

You've got a problem!

If the company is going to make my short-term bonus pensionable, how about making my long-term bonus pensionable as well?

There's no reason why that couldn't be done. But hardly any companies have gone that far to date. Among other things, the extra costs involved could be quite high. Moreover, if a decent percentage of the total of your base salary, your annual bonus, and your long-term incentive bonus is paid in the form of a pension, the resulting pension could well be much larger than your final salary itself. Some would argue that such an arrangement would tempt executives to head for the nearest beach as soon as they could.

What can be done about the fact that, in changing jobs, I often lose some pension benefits?

A person can lose benefits in at least two ways when he or she changes jobs. First, the person may not be fully vested in the former company's pension plan. And so there is an outright loss of benefits.

A second problem, and one that is harder to see, can occur when a person leaves with a vested retirement benefit. To illustrate, assume that your former employer offers a pension equal to 2 percent of final five-year average salary for each year of service. You joined the company when you were twenty-five and remained until you were forty. At that time you left and became vested in a benefit equal to 30 percent (15 years × 2 percent per year) of your final average salary. You then joined your current company, which, as it turns out, has the same identical pension plan—2 percent of final five-year average salary for each year of service. Assuming you stay until age sixty-five, you will receive from this second employer a pension benefit equal to 50 percent of your final average salary (25 years × 2 percent per year). So, considering the benefits from both plans, you will end up receiving 80 percent of your final five-year average salary, right?

Wrong! Let's assume your final five-year average salary at the time of your retirement is $300,000. To be sure, you will receive from your current employer a benefit of $150,000, or 50 percent of this $300,000 final average salary. But the benefit from your earlier employer will not be predicated on your $300,000 final five-year average salary at the time of your retirement, but rather on the average salary you earned during your last five years of service with that earlier employer. On that basis, your average pay might be a paltry $50,000, and, therfore, you might end up receiving a second pension benefit of only $15,000. As a result, you end up with a total pension of $165,000, which, instead of being the 80 percent of your final five-year average salary that you thought you'd be receiving, ends up being only 55 percent.

How can I get around a pension loss if I switch employers?

A few companies have an extra goodie built into their SERPs. They recognize that sometimes a talented executive who changes jobs never spends enough time at any single company to generate a decent-sized pension benefit. So they adopt one of several approaches.

First, the company might build a lusher retirement formula into its SERP to take account of short-service executives. For example, the company with the 2 percent-per-year regular plan might indicate in its SERP that the minimum benefit payable under the SERP after fifteen years of service is not 30 percent of final pay but rather a higher 50 percent of final pay. Such a feature doesn't provide any extra benefit to an executive who has worked for the company for more than twenty-five years, but it does fortify the benefits for those with lesser amounts of service.

Another, but more uncommon approach, would be for the company to pretend in its SERP that you had been employed with the company from a date that is substantially earlier than the date you actually joined the company. For example, the company might tell you: For purposes of our SERP, you will be considered to have joined the company on a date ten years earlier than your actual date of employment. Hence, given our 2 percent-per-year formula, you will end up receiving an additional 20 percent of your final average salary. However, should you receive any pension benefits from an earlier employer that are based on the same ten years of service for which we are now giving you credit, you will have to pay over such benefits to the company up to the amount of the extra benefit we are giving you.

Suppose the company forces me into early retirement before I have had an opportunity to build up any substantial pension. Is there any relief offered here?

In some companies, there is. Such relief usually comes in the SERP and may take different forms. For example, the company may waive any actuarial discounts in the event of an early retirement and, in effect, start paying you now what you would ordinarily have had to wait until age sixty-five to receive. Some other companies offer a substantial minimum retirement benefit, provided you have worked with the company for at least *x* years. (When you think about it, a minimum benefit of, say, 50 percent of final pay after, say, fifteen years of service not only helps the executive who joins the company late and stays until his or her normal retirement date but also the executive who joins the company early and is forced into early retirement.)

OK, you've sold me on a supplemental executive retirement plan. How do I sign up?

You don't. Most SERPs work on an invitation-only basis. In many companies, the eligibility criterion is based on salary grade; any executive assigned to salary grade 15, or say, higher is automatically eligible for the SERP. In other companies, the criterion may relate to whether or not you are an officer. And in still other companies, choices are made on a purely case-by-case basis. But in almost all companies, the number of executives invited to join the SERP is relatively small.

*I hear that some companies offer extra
amounts of life insurance to their more
senior executives. Is that true?*

Yes, at least in a number of companies. The typical company these days offers all its salaried employees life insurance as a multiple of the employee's salary. Thus, the company may offer each employee life insurance in the amount of twice the employee's current salary. The company may foot the entire bill for the insurance, or the employee may be asked to share some of the cost.

In a number of companies, however, a decision is made to supplement the regular life insurance coverage and extend greater amounts of coverage to more senior executives. For example, although the company may offer coverage equal to twice salary for all but company officers, company officers receive coverage equal to four times salary.

*What form does the extra life insurance
coverage take?*

In some instances, the extra coverage is simply additional group life insurance—the very same type of insurance offered to employees generally. However, many insurance carriers will not write group life insurance policies beyond a certain individual insurance limit. In those cases, the method of choice for funding the extra life insurance is something called *split-dollar* life insurance.

What's "split-dollar life insurance"?

Under the typical plan, the company purchases what is essentially an ordinary whole life insurance policy on the executive's life. Then the premium for the insurance policy is split between the company and the executive, with the former paying a large portion or all of that part of the premium equal to the increase in cash values, and the latter paying the remainder—the portion that represents the true cost of insurance. Should the executive die, the company takes out of the proceeds of the policy the cash surrender value and remits the remainder to the executive's estate.

Am I wrong in assuming that split-dollar life insurance is not all that great a deal for the executive?

That may well be the case, since the executive is paying all the costs of the true insurance. Nonetheless, if that is the only way extra insurance can be obtained, at least the executive does not have to lay out his or her own funds for the entire premium cost.

How about offering greater amounts of insurance coverage after retirement?

That seems to be a growing trend for more senior executives. Under most ordinary group life insurance plans applicable to all employees, insurance coverage drops rapidly after retirement until it reaches some small sum like, say, $5000. The purpose of this sum, although it isn't talked about in polite company, is simply to make sure there are funds with which to bury you.

In recent years, some companies have started to provide much greater amounts of post-retirement life insurance coverage to senior executives. Indeed, some companies do not cut the insurance coverage at all when the executive retires. So if the executive is receiving twice his or her salary in life insurance coverage while still employed, he or she will receive the same dollar amount of insurance at retirement.

Sooner or later, of course, that post-retirment life insurance is going to have to pay out. So from that standpoint, you can look at any post-retirement life insurance coverage (beyond the minimum burial expense) as being a company contribution to your estate. If, say, the company continues $500,000 of life insurance past your retirement, then when you finally die, your estate will receive $500,000 from the insurance carrier.

Recognizing this, one large commercial bank with such a post-retirement insurance arrangement offers an eligible executive the choice of cancelling his or her insurance coverage upon retirement and receiving instead a life annuity equal to the current value of the insurance coverage.

What are the tax consequences of supplemental life insurance?

Current tax law provides that you can receive tax-free only $50,000 of life insurance. Any life insurance above that amount that is not paid for by you generates what is known as *imputed income*, that is, amounts that you must take into your ordinary income and pay tax on.

The amount of imputed income that you are required to recognize in any year is a function of two variables, the amount of life insurance in excess of $50,000 for which you have not paid the cost and your age. In effect, the IRS publishes a table showing the imputed income value per $1000 of life insurance coverage for various age groups. The older you are, the higher is the imputed income charge.

When this imputed income concept was first introduced, insurance experts were of the opinion that the IRS table for imputed income constituted a deal for the executive. That is to say, what the IRS claimed were the costs of the extra insurance did not equal what you would truly have to pay a life insurance carrier to provide the same level of coverage.

However, in recent years, many insurance experts have reversed their opinion and now contend that the IRS table charges you too much for your added life insurance coverage. This is because people are living longer and premiums therefore do not need to be as high.

SUPPLEMENTAL MEDICAL INSURANCE

Do some companies offer extra medical insurance only to their executives?

Yes. Until recently, there was a growing trend to do just that. Under a typical supplemental medical insurance plan, the company told selected executives: Submit to us all the medical and dental bills incurred by you and your dependents. We will first reimburse you under our regular group medical insurance plan for whatever that plan provides. Then, if you have not been reimbursed in full, we will give you a second check to cover any excess costs.

***Am I right in assuming that most regular
medical insurance plans pick up virtually all
medical costs and that, therefore, there
really is little need to have a supplemental
medical insurance plan for executives?***

No, not necessarily. It may be true that your group medical insurance plan pays expenses above a small deductible, for example, $300 per year for you and your family. And it may be true that the plan pays 100 percent of all hospital costs up to, say, 120 days. And it may be true that your plan pays 100 percent of a reasonable surgical schedule. And it may be true that your plan pays 80 percent of all other costs. But consider that:

- You may require an extra-long hospital stay and hence have to pay 20 percent of the incremental costs yourself.
- Your surgeon may charge more than the normal fee, again requiring you to pick up 20 percent of the extra costs.
- If you or your dependents require psychiatric care, you may find that your plan offers no reimbursement at all. Or perhaps it only picks up 50 percent of the costs, and then only up to a nominal amount per visit.
- You may find that vision care costs are not covered at all.
- You will find that physical examination costs are not covered.
- Dental insurance coverage is likely to be either nonexistent or not very liberal. For example, the plan may pay no more than 50 percent of the costs up to a fairly tight limit.

You can see that there are plenty of holes in any group medical insurance plan and that, therefore, a supplemental medical insurance plan can represent quite an attractive benefit for many executives.

***Is there any tax advantage to supplemental
medical insurance?***

Yes. Here's one of the few cases where an outright tax advantage can be obtained. To illustrate, let us start with the tax law in effect prior to 1984 and let us take the case of an executive whose adjusted gross income is $300,000 and who, in a particular year, has incurred

$3000 of drug costs in excess of those reimbursed under his normal group insurance plan and has also incurred $9000 of medical costs in excess of those reimbursed under his normal group insurance plan.

He now goes to file his taxes. When it comes to the medical expense section of his tax return, he finds he is asked to list his excess drug expenses. He promptly writes down the $3000 figure. Next, he is asked to enter 1 percent of his adjusted gross income, a figure that turns out to be $3000. Finally, he is asked to deduct the second figure from the first figure. The answer is zero, and that is how much of the $3000 of excess drug expenses he is allowed to deduct.

The tax return then asks him to list his excess medical expenses other than drug expenses. He enters here the $9000 he spent. Next, he is asked to enter a figure equal to 3 percent of his adjusted gross income, which in this case is $9000. Finally, he is again asked to deduct the second figure from the first. Once again, he has been defeated in his attempt to obtain any medical expense deductions.

In this example, the executive spent $12,000 out of his pocket on medical expenses and was not reimbursed under his regular group insurance plan; and not one dollar ended up being deductible.

One way the company could solve this problem for the executive would be to give him an additional bonus of $24,000. Then, after paying taxes at a 50 percent rate, he would be left with the $12,000 required to pay himself back for the excess medical expenses he incurred. But there is a more cost-efficient method available to the company: Establish a supplemental medical insurance plan and give the executive a check for $12,000 under that plan. That way, the executive incurs no tax on the $12,000 payment and therefore gets to keep all of it. At a stroke, the company has spent only half as much money to put a given sum in the executive's pocket.

In some ways, things get worse in tax years starting in 1984 or later. Now you don't have to deduct 1 percent of your adjusted gross income from your drug expenses. That's the good news. But after summing your drug and medical expenses, you then have to deduct 5 percent of your adjusted gross income, not 3 percent. And that is decidedly the bad news.

If supplemental medical insurance is such a good deal, why doesn't every company have a supplemental medical insurance plan for its executives?

Two reasons. First, anything relating to illness can become an emotional issue. Although many workers do not begrudge Mr. Big his high salary and bonus (because, among other things, they hope their own children will have an opportunity to become Mr. or Ms. Big in the next generation), they surely would have a hard time understanding why Mr. Big should have 100 percent of his medical insurance costs reimbursed, while they should have only 80 percent reimbursed. Indeed, to them, equity would, in effect, suggest that the reimbursement ratios be switched.

Accordingly, a company adopting a supplemental medical insurance plan and limiting it to a handful of senior executives (which is almost always the case) is going to have a potential public relations problem.

At the same time, the company has to contend with a changed tax law. Some years ago, President Carter attempted to revise the tax law to provide that reimbursements under medical insurance plans would not escape taxation unless the plan provided equal coverage to all employees, and not merely to highly paid executives. He did not achieve his goal, but, curiously, the Congress did write a provision into the law which provided that tax-free reimbursement could only be made under a plan written with an insurance carrier (as opposed to being self-insured, which was the usual method prior to the change in the law).

At first, companies found it hard to find a carrier willing to write such coverage, given the small group of executives involved and the fact that none of them were to be given any incentive to hold down their medical expenses. However, as time passed, the free market did serve up some carriers ready to write the coverage. So, today, it is possible to sidestep this provision of the law, although the cost of the coverage may be a limiting factor.

How do I convince my company to grant me an employment contract?

Be terribly silver-tongued! The fact is that few executives in the U.S. work under employment contracts, except in the entertainment industry. However, the incidence of employment contracts is growing, rather than shrinking, even if the absolute number of executives covered is still quite low.

What rights does an employment contract give me?

There are all sorts of employment contracts. The most simple type of contract provides only that you will be employed by the company for x years at a salary of not less than y. It also states that if you are thrown out the door, except for strict cause (say, theft), the company will pay you a sum equal to your salary for the time remaining in your contract. Viewed from that perspective, this type of contract is nothing more than an individualized severance pay agreement.

However, contracts can get much more exotic. For openers, the contract might provide that it is not enough for the company merely to employ you for x years at y salary per year. Rather, you must be employed as, say, chief financial officer, or in a higher position, and you must be located in, say, New York. Should the company demote you and/or should the company move you to Houston, you have a right to resign your employment and yet still receive your salary for the remainder of your contract term.

Next, the contract may provide that your salary will be increased according to a predetermined schedule during each year in the contract life. For example, the contract may provide something along these lines: Your initial salary will be $250,000 per year. Upon each anniversary of the execution of this contract, your salary will be increased by the percentage change in the Consumer Price Index. In addition, after making this adjustment, your salary shall be increased by a further 3 percent.

In this case, therefore, the executive is being guaranteed a real (i.e., discounted for inflation) increase in salary of 3 percent per year.

Next, the contract may provide for how your bonus will be determined. For example, you may be promised a bonus according to a predetermined formula. One executive was told: A bonus fund for all executives in your subsidiary shall be determined, with said fund equal to 10 percent of all pretax profits of the subsidiary less an amount equal to 15 percent of the subsidiary's beginning-of-the-year capital employed. Once the fund is determined, you shall receive a payment equal to 25 percent of the fund.

The contract may go on to spell out in detail the long-term incentive grants the executive will receive during the term of the contract. And it may provide for special vacation allowances, special benefits, and/or special perquisites.

Sometimes, a contract also provides for various types of special bonuses. For example, there may be a so-called *signing* bonus—upon signing the contract, the executive receives a check for, say, $100,000. Or the executive may be promised a *back end* bonus: If he or she remains with the company for the life of the contract, he or she then receives a check for $100,000. Or the executive may be promised a guaranteed minimum bonus. For example: Your annual bonus will be determined in accordance with the judgment of the Compensation Committee of the Board. We contemplate that, in a year of normal performance, you will receive a bonus approximating 50 percent of your salary. And we also contemplate that, for truly outstanding performance, you could receive a bonus of up to 100 percent of your salary. However, in no event will your bonus in any year of this contract be less than 25 percent of your salary, or $100,000, whichever is the greater amount.

In summary, therefore, an employment agreement can run to 2 pages or to 200 pages.

Why are there so few employment contracts around?

There are a number of reasons. First, working without a contract has always fitted in with the macho image that many executives have of themselves. Second, extending a contract to an executive raises equity questions—especially in a volatile industry where the ordinary workers can be thrown out in the street at will and be given hardly anything.

But the biggest impediment probably lies in the one-way-street nature of employment contracts. Should the company breach the contract, the executive will find the courts quite sympathetic to making the company pay for its breach. But should the executive breach the contract (e.g., by quitting), the courts may be loath to impose substantial penalties on him or her. You sometimes read of a company hauling a former executive into court and trying to obtain damages because the executive has quit and joined a competitor. But it is often the case that the court will take pity on the executive and not impose damages. And because this is so, some companies don't even bother to sue an executive who has breached an employment contract. Understandably, those same companies are leery when it comes to granting the replacement executive an employment contract.

GOLDEN PARACHUTE AGREEMENTS

What is a golden parachute agreement?

It is a special form of employment contract—one that is activated only if what the lawyers call a *change of control* occurs.

What constitutes a change of control?

Under the most conservative approach, a change of control is not deemed to occur unless some party, not previously in the picture, acquires more than 50 percent of your company's stock. However, a more liberal approach might stipulate that a change of control has occurred if only, say, 20 percent of the stock has been so acquired. Or, in other cases, change of control is defined in terms of seats on the board of directors. For example, if the majority of faces now around the boardroom table are not the same faces who were around the table eighteen months earlier, a change of control has been deemed to occur.

What happens if there is a change of control?

In some cases, once a change of control has occurred, the executive is free to pull the ripcord on his or her golden parachute and terminate employment with the company. If he or she does, all sorts of nice things may happen. In other cases, the ripcord won't work unless there is both a change of control and what is known as a constructive discharge.

What's a constructive discharge?

Suppose your company is acquired in a hostile takeover situation. One way the new owners can get rid of you is simply to fire you. That constitutes an outright discharge and will doubtless trigger your golden parachute agreement, thereby costing the new owners plenty.

Suppose, however, that they want to get you to quit so that they can get off the hook. They can, for example, demote you to a lower-level position and broadcast widely the fact that they think you are a dog. Or they can move your office to Anchorage. Or they can keep you in the same building but relocate your office to a stairwell. Or they can cut your salary. Finally, when you become fed up enough, you quit and they point benignly to your decision to quit as proof that you weren't fired.

Contemplating that such behavior could occur, the drafters of golden parachute agreements coined the term *constructive discharge* to apply to resignations induced by certain types of actions taken by the company. In such cases, the executive is considered to have been constructively discharged, even though he or she has not actually been discharged. That being the case, all the benefits applicable to an actual discharge become available to the executive.

Conditions triggering a constructive discharge typically relate to your keeping the same or an equivalent-level position, not having your salary cut, and not being involuntarily relocated to another city.

What benefits are payable when the ripcord is finally pulled?

Benefits vary tremendously. Looking at the most liberal benefit packages, we find the executive receiving his or her salary for five years after termination. Moreover, short-term incentive awards continue to be paid, and at maximum, not normal, levels. Finally, maximum long-term incentive payments are also made. If the executive gets another position within a few months after pulling the ripcord, he or she ends up receiving two compensation packages at once.

On the other hand, the most conservative companies using golden parachute agreements (the really conservative companies don't use them at all), may offer the executive only two years' salary past termination. And bonuses and long-term incentive payouts are paid at more normal levels, not at maximum levels. Finally, should the executive find other employment during the two-year period, then any compensation he or she receives from the second employer is deducted from the amounts owed by the first employer.

Who receives golden parachute agreements?

Normally, such agreements are extended only to the most senior executives of a company. The theory is that these people are the most vulnerable when their company is taken over by another company—especially if they fought the takeover and thereby caused the acquiring company to have to pay more than otherwise might have been thé case.

Are payments received under golden parachute contracts taxed the same way as other forms of compensation?

You would certainly think so, assuming there is any logic to the tax code. But as we all know, there isn't.

Until 1984, payments under golden parachute agreements were indeed treated in the same manner as normal compensation payments. But then the law changed, owing to the fact that many people had concluded that companies were acting outrageously in their desire to protect executives.

Under the new tax law, nothing special happens if the present value (i.e., after discounting payments to be made in the future to account for the time value of money) of a golden parachute contract is less than three times an executive's so-called base compensation amount. In turn, the base compensation amount is the average annual compensation (including base salary, annual bonus, option profits, and so forth) he has received during the five years preceding the change of control.

But let the present value of the golden parachute equal or exceed three times the base compensation amount, and all hell breaks loose. First, the company is denied its tax deduction—not merely on the excess over three times the base compensation amount, but on the excess over one times the base compensation amount. Even worse, the executive ends up having to pay a 20 percent excise tax—again, on the excess over the base compensation amount.

To illustrate, take an executive whose base compensation amount is $300,000. If the present value of his golden parachute turns out to be $899,999, he pays no extra tax. But if it turns out to be $900,000, the entire excess of $900,000 over the base compensation amount of $300,000, or $600,000, attracts a 20 percent excise tax. So, in this case, the hapless executive ends up paying an extra tax of $120,000 on just one dollar more income. That's some marginal tax rate, don't you think?

If you have a golden parachute agreement, you should analyze its provisions carefully to determine whether you are likely to have to pay any excise tax should the agreement be triggered, as well as the amount of such tax. If it looks as though you will come out behind, you ought to ask your employer to agree to a modification of the agreement that will save you—and the company—money.

SECTION FIVE

PERQUISITES

Contrary to popular belief, American executives are not generally awash with perquisites. But there are some goodies out there to be had. Did you know that:

- Although there may not be much of a tax advantage to having a company car, you'll probably reap a real tax advantage if you can convince your company to forget about the car and instead give you a car and a driver.
- Many companies pay to have your balance sheet analyzed by experts and the best of investment advice provided.
- Quite a few companies will authorize you to use the company's outside auditors to prepare your tax return and then pick up the entire tab.
- Some companies will even see that you don't have to pay anything for any legal work you require (except perhaps for suing the company!).

What is the IRS's attitude toward perquisites?

Ambivalent, to say the least. On the one hand, the IRS would love to apply its doctrine of economic benefit to anything having a tangible economic benefit. On the other hand, the IRS knows that if it did so, it might spark a taxpayer revolution, with the result that total tax collections, instead of rising, might drop. Remember that perquisites are really not confined to senior executives; rather, they are found throughout our society. Low-level employees of retail establishments typically receive discounts on any purchases they make from their employer. Airline employees of all ranks are permitted to fly for little or nothing—and throughout the world, to boot. And many middle-level executives are tacitly permitted to use company phones for personal long-distance calls, as well as to have their secretaries prepare personal letters for them.

In recent years, thoughtful people at the IRS (don't be surprised, there really are some!), as well as certain members of Congress, have tried to find some sort of middle-ground approach to the problem. They are trying to exempt from taxation any perquisite that meets two conditions. First, the perquisite must be granted, to employees generally, not merely to executives. And second, the perquisite must carry little or no cost to the employer. Here, for example, free travel for airline employees would be exempt from taxation, because it is not just executives who are extended the privilege; moreover, the incremental costs of letting an employee use a seat that the airline was not able to sell are very low.

On the other hand, a perquisite extended only to executives, whether it carries little cost or a lot of cost, would be fair game for the IRS.

What's the IRS's attitude toward company cars?

This is the most sought after of all perquisites—the most sought after by the executive and the most sought after by the IRS, too!

The IRS's position is quite clear on company cars. To illustrate, assume that you have been furnished a company-leased car, with the lease cost being $600 per month. Assume further that the company also pays for gasoline and other miscellaneous items as well, and that these amount to another $100 per month. All in all, the costs are therefore $700 per month. Finally, assume that you use the car only for personal purposes and do not drive it on business at all. Remember that the IRS always takes the position that driving from home to work and return is never considered a business trip.

When you file your tax return, you will find that you have to include in your ordinary income the entire $8400 of economic benefit. The formula is as follows. First, you determine the total cost of the car ($8400); then you multiply the total cost by a fraction, the numerator of which is the total miles you drove the car during the year for personal purposes and the denominator of which is the total miles you drove for any purposes. In our example, all the miles were personal miles, and so the value of the fraction is 1. Hence, when you multiply $8400 by 1, you get $8400. (Alternatively, had you driven the car only 50 percent of the time for personal purposes, the value of the fraction would be 0.5, and you would have included a lesser $4200 in your ordinary income.) So in this case, you ended up paying ordinary income tax on the entire value of the company car.

Even if I have to pay some tax for a company car, don't I still come out ahead?

Not really. Let's review the transaction for a moment. First, the company shelled out $8400 for the car (leaving aside the fact that it can deduct this $8400 amount and receive something back from the government). And, assuming you are at the maximum 50 percent ordinary tax rate, you paid the government $4200. Also assume that your after-tax pay from salary and bonus was $80,000 in that particular year. Hence, you ended up with net cash of $80,000—$4200, or $75,800— plus a car.

Now assume, alternatively, that your company tires of giving you a car. Rather, it tells you: Look, we were spending $84000 a year on you before, so we'll simply give you an extra bonus payment of $8400, and you do with it what you want.

In this case, your net cash from the company increases. First, you have the $80,000 net after-tax cash from your salary and bonus. Then you also have the $8400 additional bonus. However, this is taxable at 50 percent, so you realize only $4200 of it. Nonetheless, your final net cash becomes $80,000 + $4200, or $84,200.

But you no longer have a car. So you go down to your friendly leasing agency and lease a car yourself. You pay $600 per month to the leasing agency and spend another $100 per month on gasoline and other miscellaneous items. Hence, your total costs are the same $8400 per year as experienced previously. Since none of these costs were incurred in connection with business pursuits, you are not permitted any tax deductions. The result is that you are out of pocket by $8400. After deducting this $8400 expenditure from your $84,200 of net cash, we find that you are left with—guess what?—$75,800 of net cash and a car. And that is exactly the same position you were in when you had a company car.

To sum up, it's better to have a company car than to have nothing extra, even if you have to pay $4200 in taxes. But if the company is willing to give you in cash what it was spending on the car, you are likely to come out even.

Is there any limit to the type of car the company can give me?

The company can give you Cleopatra's barge if it wishes, but under a law passed in 1984, its ability to take advantage of the Investment Tax

Credit and to use accelerated depreciation is limited to the extent the car is relatively expensive (e.g., in the BMV, Mercedes, and Rolls class).

As a result of these changes, the true cost to the company to buy or lease a luxury car has been increased. In turn, that means that you will have to increase the amount you take into your income for your personal use of that car.

But if you use the car only for company business, and the company doesn't mind incurring some extra cost, you can tool around town in your Rolls with nary a care in the world.

Even if there is no legitimate tax advantage to having a company car, the company can still get a better leasing deal than I can, can't it?

You're right. There may well be a volume purchase advantage to having the company make the transaction. And from that standpoint, if the company gave you the cash it was spending and you tried to duplicate the transaction, you might find yourself coming out short. But a volume purchasing advantage is not a tax advantage. So far, we haven't seen any sort of tax advantage to a company car.

Are you sure there's no way I can get a tax advantage from a company car? I simply can't believe there's no way to get there.

Well, you can always be a little forgetful as to just how many of the miles you drove during the year were personal miles. So maybe it wasn't the case that all 20,000 of the miles were personal miles. Maybe only 10,000 miles were personal miles. And if you're wrong, well, nobody's perfect!

In fact, it is in this area where there is a true tax advantage. But we are dealing with tax *evasion*, not with tax avoidance. Once you cross that line, there's a whole world of interesting possibilities—and a fairly wide range of penalties as well!

I heard that you can get around these tax problems by having your company deduct something each month to represent your personal use of the company car. Won't that work?

Many people, and many companies as well, believe that if you are seen to be paying some nominal sum for imputed personal use of the car, you won't have to pay anything extra. For example, one company tells its executives: We are going to deduct $100 per month from your pay as reimbursement for the fact that you use your company car part of the time for personal reasons, as opposed to business reasons.

In other cases, the company may deduct nothing. Rather, it adds an amount to your W-2 income to represent the personal use of the car. Then you pay tax on that added amount.

Will either approach hold the IRS at bay? Ironically, it may, if for no other reason than that the IRS did get a few ounces of flesh, if not a full pound. And, given the time it takes to look through company records to see who has a company car and then to perform individual audits on each executive to see if he or she fairly reported the car, maybe those few ounces represent a reasonable outcome.

From a strictly legal standpoint, the fact that your company charged you $100 per month for your company car or added $100 per month to your W-2 statement means nothing. Once again, the only pertinent fact is the percentage of time you used the car for personal purposes.

If what you say is true, then Mr. Big must pay a fortune to have that huge limo take him to and from work, right?

Wrong! We have a bit of an irony here. You would think that if the costs of commuting to and from work are not deductible, then Mr. Big would end up paying a whopping cost for the use of a chauffeured limousine to pick him up each morning and then to deposit him home each evening.

But Mr. Big can be expected to come up with interesting arguments as to why he should pay no taxes for the use of the limousine. The arguments assert that the limo is there not for his personal use and enjoyment, but rather because his employer insists it be there. First, he is able to use the limousine to review confidential papers that he would never let see the light of day in a public conveyance. Second, since he doesn't have to have his hands on a steering wheel and his eyes on the road, he can do other things besides review papers—make telephone calls and even have business meetings with some of his subordinates. Finally, since there is some risk that someone will want to do Mr. Big in (perhaps an irate shareholder!), the limousine provides a measure of personal security, compared to a train or a car Mr. Big drives himself.

And to prove that, the company will point out that the chauffeur just finished taking a course on how to make a 180-degree turn on one wheel while simultaneously pushing Mr. Big down on to his plushly carpeted rear (the rear of the car, that is).

In a few cases, however, the company will make some sort of charge to the executive for use of the limousine in commuting to and from work. One New York company, for example, charges its CEO an amount equal to what he would have paid to purchase a train ticket on Conrail. Here again, we have the implicit argument that the extra economic benefit relating to the limousine is for the convenience of the company, not for the convenience of the executive.

So I suppose that flying in the corporate jet is also tax-free, isn't it?

Most likely. Clearly, using the corporate jet for a valid business purpose is not a taxable event. It may well be that this is one plane you don't mind sitting in the back of, but, nonetheless, the purpose is business and there is no tax to pay.

Suppose, however, that Mr. Big takes along his wife on a business trip. Will he have to pay taxes in this instance?

That depends. If he can show that his wife's presence is important for business purposes, then the costs of her trip can be reimbursed on a tax-free basis. Otherwise, anything paid by the company should technically be included in the executive's income.

An interesting sidebar involves just what the costs of spouse travel are when the company jet is being used. For example, assume that the CEO is flying from New York to Los Angeles on the company jet and that there are plenty of empty seats. So he takes his wife along purely for personal reasons. Now what is the cost of her trip? Is it, for example, the value of a round-trip first class commercial air ticket? Or is it the value of a round-trip economy class commercial air ticket, given that she is sitting in the back of the plane? Or is it the cost that the CEO would incur to charter a corporate jet for the same trip? Or is it the true incremental costs that the company incurs with respect to the wife's travel? In this last instance, the company could reason that no charge should be made for the capital costs of the jet, since these were incurred fundamentally for business purposes. Likewise, no charge should be made for the pilots' compensation, since they have to be paid whether or not the wife travels. Indeed, from that perspective, the only extra costs incurred for the wife's travel turn out to be the sixty extra gallons of fuel expended because of the added weight, the steak dinner, and the bottle of Bordeaux wine—a total cost of $80.

Different companies, and different IRS agents, too, will come up with different answers to this question.

What's the status of country clubs?

The IRS is particularly hard when it comes to trying to deduct the costs of a country club membership and/or to avoid paying taxes if the company foots the bill. Not only are deductions limited to business use of the country club, but no deductions at all are allowed unless the business use constitutes more than 50 percent of the total use of the club. Hence, if my country club dues and fees are, say, $3000 per year, and if I play golf there 100 times in a year, with 45 of the times being business-related, and the remainder being personal, then I may deduct nothing. Yet, if 51 of the times were business-related then I could deduct 51 percent of the total cost, or $1530.

How about luncheon clubs?

Here's one area where the IRS is pretty lenient. First of all, you don't have to show that more than 50 percent of the use of the luncheon club was business-related. Indeed, you don't have to show much of any-thing, because executive luncheon clubs are rarely, if ever, used for anything other than strictly business purposes.

How about physical examinations?

Many companies provide free annual physical examinations for members of their executive group. These examinations can be quite comprehensive—indeed, excruciatingly comprehensive! And the costs can run into the hundreds of dollars per executive per year.

If you qualify for the executive physical examination program, you should have no problems with the IRS, even though it could, in theory, impute income to you to the extent of the costs of the physical examination. Basically, the IRS seems inclined to accept the argument that the physical examination is for the benefit of the company as much as it is for the benefit of the executive.

What about personal financial counseling?

In the 1960s, companies began to discover that otherwise financially sophisticated executives were making a botch of their personal financial affairs. It wasn't that the executive didn't know what to do; he or she simply didn't have the time to do it. Accordingly, companies started to retain the services of professional advisors who could help executives get their personal financial affairs in order and then start to make wise investment choices.

At first, personal financial counseling was overlooked by the IRS, and no executive paid a tax on services received. But then the IRS issued a ruling requiring companies to include the costs of personal financial counseling in the executive's W-2 statement. As a result, if you are furnished services for which the company pays $3000, the sum of $3000 is added to your W-2 statement, and you are required to include this $3000 sum in your ordinary income.

That being the case, you would end up paying taxes on the $3000 were it not for the fact that a large part of the cost is deductible, for example, tax counseling. Hence, what really happens with personal financial counseling is that you end up paying tax on a small fraction of the costs defrayed by your company.

Who generally receives personal financial counseling?

Typically, personal financial counseling is extended to few executives in a company—perhaps those who are officers and a few others.

In the case of lower-level executives, some companies offer a variant of personal financial counseling—group financial counseling. Thus, they will convene executives in small groups and pay for experts to address the group and answer questions.

Do some companies pay for tax counseling?

Yes. It is not uncommon for a company to permit its senior executives to use the tax services of its outside auditors. These tax experts then advise the executive on tax shelters and other tax matters and also assist the executive in the preparation of his or her tax return.

If I receive tax counseling, do I have to pay a tax on the benefits involved?

No. If you were required to include the tax counseling costs in your ordinary income, you would turn right around and take a like deduction. The costs of tax counseling, after all, are fully tax-deductible.

What about general legal counseling?

A few companies permit senior executives to use the services of the company's outside law firm. Here, the executive receives, not necessarily tax advice, but general legal advice.

In theory, the costs of such services, excluding any of the services related to tax matters, ought to be included in the executive's ordinary income. But it is difficult to tell whether companies are in fact adding the costs of such services to the executive's W-2 statement.

Some companies give their executives lush expense allowances. What happens here?

There's no question that some companies are more liberal than others when it comes to reimbursing expenses. Thus, one company will permit you to fly first class and rent a suite in an exclusive hotel, while the second company will have you flying in the back of the plane and then looking for the cheapest hotel room you can find. In both cases, all the expenses incurred are not taxable to the executive, provided there is a clear business purpose involved.

Some other companies give their executives an outright expense allowance. In one company, it is understood that the executive will document any ordinary and necessary business expenses on his or her expense report. Then the company pays the executive $50,000 per year on top of the documented expenses. Such an approach simply results in extra ordinary income for the executive. Paying $50,000 as a special expense allowance or paying $50,000 as extra bonus makes no difference to the IRS—cash is cash, no matter what you call it.

Suppose I spend more on business-related expenses than my company will reimburse me for. Can I deduct the excess on my expense report?

Yes, you can. But you'd better be prepared for an audit. Let's go back to the executive who is forced by his company to fly coach and to rent cheap hotel rooms. Our executive, not finding this humble lifestyle to his taste, pays out of his own pocket the funds necessary to upgrade his air ticket to first class and to obtain a suite in an exclusive hotel. He then deducts the out-of-pocket costs on his income tax return, claiming they were ordinary and necessary business expenses not reimbursed by his employer. And he doesn't think there will be a problem because, after all, his friend Bill, who works for a truly open-handed company is routinely reimbursed for all the same level of expenses and has never had a problem with the IRS.

Unfortunately, such will not likely be the case here. The IRS may well come sniffing around and will then probably mount this Catch-22 argument: Your employer refused to reimburse you for first-class air travel and for renting a suite in a hotel. Therefore, your employer does not see these extra expenses as being necessary to your business travel. So if your employer doesn't see them as being necessary, what makes you think we, the IRS, should be more charitable?

Keeping this in mind, you should make every effort to have your company reimburse you for any business-related expense. If necessary, it would be better to have the company foot the bill and then reduce your bonus by a like amount. In that manner, you will not be in the position of trying to convince the IRS that the excess expenses for which your company would not give you a dime really do constitute ordinary and necessary business expenses.

When you add together the true value of all perquisites, what are they really worth?

In most cases, not all that much. Those who don't have any perquisites often fantasize about the value of all the perquisites that top executives receive. But, first, there aren't that many in most companies. And second, if you look only at the nonbusiness-related portions of perquisites, the totals are almost minuscule in relation to the overall size of the executive compensation package. Consider, for example, a CEO with a base salary of $500,000, an annual bonus of $250,000, long-term incentive payouts of another $500,000, and fringe benefits worth $150,000. We have a package of $1.4 million per year. Now suppose that, after stripping away the business-related portions, the true value of all his perquisites comes to $15,000 per year. That turns out to represent just a fraction over 1 percent of his total compensation package. And even if you doubled that figure to $30,000 per year—a highly unlikely level of perquisite expenditure—the perquisite package would represent only around 2 percent of the total compensation package.

Other countries give a lot more perquisites than we do. Why is that?

Perquisites tend to thrive in the soil of high taxation. If a country taxes income at confiscatory rates (e.g., a marginal tax rate of 90 percent), then there is a much greater incentive to try and find ways to deliver income in a form that is not taxed. This has been the case in England, where, until recently, the maximum tax rate on ordinary income was greater than 80 percent. And it was certainly the case in the U.S. where, prior to 1964, the maximum tax rate on ordinary income was 91 percent.

But now in the U.S. we have a maximum ordinary tax rate of 50 percent. That may seem like a high rate to those paying it, but compared to many other countries, it is a breeze. And because the rate is so relatively low, and also because the IRS is fairly vigilant when it comes to spotting and taxing perquisites, many companies have rightly taken the stance of holding down on perquisites and simply paying a lot of cash.

THE COMPENSATION COMMITTEE

Herewith, a few words on a sometimes-unnoticed group of worthies who, if they are not asleep, can have a highly significant impact on what you receive and when you receive it. And these days, most of them are not asleep!

What is a compensation committee?

Almost all publicly owned companies have formed a committee comprised of outside directors (i.e., nonemployee directors) to ride herd on the company's compensation levels. Typically, the committee contains three or five members, none of whom are eligible to participate in any of the company's regular compensation programs. Given that these board members cannot benefit from their actions, they are considered to be objective and therefore capable of making unbiased decisions.

What do they decide?

Typically, the committee must approve pay increases and bonus awards for all executives above a certain level. The level varies from company to company, but, normally, only corporate officers and a few highly paid nonofficers have their pay individually reviewed by the committee.

At the same time, the committee reviews and approves all compensation plans for executives generally. Hence, if the company adopts a short-term incentive plan for 300 executives, the text of the plan will have to be approved by the committee before being submitted to the full board of directors, and perhaps to the shareholders as well, for approval.

Finally, the committee may also approve such things as salary increase budgets, although this use of a committee is relatively uncommon.

What impact does the committee have on me?

If you are one of the executives whose pay must be individually reviewed and approved by the committee, a lot of impact. After all, the committee might not agree with your CEO's recommendations. Or your CEO might want to use the committee as the fall guy for your not getting a salary increase. ("I fought tooth and nail with the committee, but they shot me down!")

However, even if your pay is not individually approved by the committee, its actions with respect to the pay of your superiors and its actions with respect to incentive plan design can have a pronounced effect on your pay—at least over time. For example, if the committee holds down the pay of the CEO, your pay may also be held down as a result of that decision.

SECTION SIX

TIPS ON CHANGING EMPLOYERS

section 9y

TIPS
OF characters

WHAT TO ASK THE PROSPECTIVE EMPLOYER

Should you find yourself considering an offer from another company, here's a list of questions to ask and things to do that should prove helpful in assessing the compensation aspects of the employer's offer. First, some questions to ask:

- Who do you consider to be your major competition in establishing your overall pay policy?
- Where do you try to come out vis-à-vis that competition? At the median? At the 75th percentile?
- To what salary grade will I be assigned?
- What is the range of my salary grade?
- What are the salary ranges of my principal subordinates and of my boss?
- How do I move from the minimum of my assigned range to the maximum of the range? Does my personal performance count, and if so, how much?
- When was the last time the entire salary structure was adjusted? What was the percentage increase applied to the structure?
- How much is the company spending on salary increases (as a percentage of payroll) this year?
- Am I eligible to participate in the company's short-term incentive program?
- What is the size of my normal award opportunity? And my maximum award opportunity?
- Is the bonus plan funded by means of some kind of formula? If so, what is the formula?

189

- Under what circumstances am I likely to receive a normal bonus award? A maximum bonus award? No bonus award at all?

- What has been the size of bonus awards as a percentage of aggregate normal awards over the past few years?

- If I am being considered for a position in a division or a subsidiary, will any portion, or even all, of my short-term incentive award opportunity be predicated on the performance of that division or subsidiary? If it will be, what happens if the division or subsidiary performs magnificently but the overall corporation falls flat on its face? Will I still receive a large incentive payout, or will the corporation's poor performance cause me to lose my entire incentive award?

- If I earn a bonus, do I get it right away or do I have to defer some portion of it?

- If I have to defer a bonus award, what happens if I resign from the company before I receive it? And will I earn any sort of return on my deferred monies?

- Is there some program of voluntary bonus deferrals available to me? If so, what are my choices?

- Will I be eligible to receive long-term incentive grants?

- What is the nature of the company's current long-term incentive plan(s)?

- If stock option grants are involved, are there any stock appreciation rights attached to my grants?

- If company stock is used in a long-term incentive plan, are the shares registered?

- If I receive company stock through the exercise of a stock option or an outright share grant, is there any pressure, subtle or not so subtle, for me to hold the shares and not sell them?

- If the company makes restricted stock grants, do I have to do anything other than stay with the company to earn out my shares?

- If the long-term incentive plan offers payouts predicated on financial performance, what are the particular goals for the most current grant? Speaking of past grants, did they pay out, or did executives earn nothing?

- If I am being considered for a position in a division or a subsidiary, will some portion, or even all, of my long-term incentive reward opportunity be predicated on the performance of that division or subsidiary? And if it will be, can I receive a payout under the plan even in the event that the overall company's performance is abysmal?

- How often are grants made?
- What is the size of a normal long-term incentive grant for someone in my position?
- What perquisites can I expect to receive? Will I have to pay any taxes on those perquisites?

Of course, you may be stonewalled on some of these questions. But there's no harm in trying to find out as much as you can.

DOING SOME HOMEWORK
ABOUT THE EMPLOYER

At the same time, you can also do a judicious bit of research yourself:

- Get hold of the company's proxy statements and annual reports for the past five years.
- Also get hold of the proxy statements of some of the company's principal competitors.
- Read the footnotes to the annual report that pertain to compensation plans. There you will find information as to the aggregate size of bonuses awarded for the particular year and the various stock option and performance unit plans.
- Read the company's proxy statements carefully. There, you will find information on how much the most senior officers received in the way of salaries and bonuses. Be sure to read all the footnotes, because you may find out more there than in the remuneration tables.
- Check the proxy statement for evidence of stock option grants, the size of grants made, and the frequency of grants made.
- Go back through several years to see if you can find the text of the current short-term and/or long-term incentive plans. If you find them, read them and make some notes.
- If you find the formulas governing the funding of short-term incentive plans and/or the goals for long-term incentive plans, construct some "what-if" scenarios and see how sensitive payouts are likely to be for varying levels of assumed future performance.
- Turn to the proxy statements of the other companies. Read them briefly and try to form some conclusions as to whether the company you are considering joining is a high payer or a chintzy one.

- Find the back issues of *Business Week* and *Forbes* that report on executive compensation payments made to the top officers of a variety of companies. Again, draw some conclusions as to the relative pay levels being offered by your prospective employer.

By asking the above questions and doing the recommended research, you will be in a much better position to evaluate whether you are being offered a good deal. At the same time, you may be in a position to assess whether those enticing short- and long-term incentive plans are indeed likely to be winners, or whether all sorts of untoward events can transpire to leave you standing in your compensation underwear.

Years ago, the Romans said it all: *Caveat emptor*—Let the buyer beware. You as the buyer of an offer being made to you by another company have the opportunity to get behind that offer, minimize the chances of a disappointment in the future, and maximize the chances that what you get in the years to come is what you thought you were going to get.

INDEX

Numbers in italics indicate graphic illustration.